MICROSOFT PUBLISHER 2024

An Updated Practical Guide for Beginner and Advanced Users

EVELYN NEUMANN

Copyright © 2024 by Evelyn Neumann
All rights reserved. This book or any portion thereof may not be reproduced or used in any manner whatsoever without the express written permission of the publisher except for the use of brief quotations in a book review.

Printed in the United States of America.

TABLE OF CONTENT

INTRODUCTION	**7**
CHAPTER ONE	**8**
BEGINNING WITH MICROSOFT PUBLISHER	**8**
CREATING A SHORTCUT FOR PUBLISHER	9
RIBBON TABS	11
THE HOME TAB	11
THE INSERT TAB	12
PAGE DESIGN TAB	12
THE MAILING TAB	13
THE REVIEW TAB	13
THE VIEW TAB	14
THE FILE BACKSTAGE	14
BUILDING A NEW DESIGN	15
CHAPTER TWO	**16**
COMMENCING WITH A NEW PUBLICATION	**16**
SIZE OF THE PUBLICATION	16
ABOUT ORIENTATION	17
ABOUT MARGINS	17
UNLOCK A NEW PUBLICATION	17
MAJOR WORKSPACE	18
HOW TO WORK WITH GUIDES	21
THE BASIC ELEMENT	21
ADDITION OF A TEXT BOX	22
HOW TO CREATE TEXT	23
LEARNING HOW TO FORMAT TEXT	23
FONT SPECIFYING	23
FONT SIZE ADJUSTMENT	24
ALTERNATING THE TEXT COLOR	26
SPECIFICATION OF TEXT ALIGNMENT	27

CHANGING OF THE CASE	29
SCANNING TYPOGRAPHY PROPERTIES	30
INCLUDING DROP CAP PROPERTIES	30
THE STYLISTIC SETS	31
THE LIGATURES	33
THE TEXT EFFECTS	34
SHADOW FEATURE	34
TEXT OUTLINE	35
WORDART STYLES	36
TEXT BOXES FORMATTING	38
BACKGROUND COLOR CHANGE	38
THE BORDERS	39
THE SHADOWS	40
THE STYLES	40
CHANGING TEXT BOXES	41
READJUSTING TEXT BOX	41
RESIZING THE TEXT BOX	42
ROTATION OF THE TEXT BOX	42
THE TEXT DIRECTION	43
TEXT AUTOFIT	43
THE TEXT BOX MARGINS	45
ALIGNING	46
HOW TO JOIN TEXT BOXES	47

CHAPTER THREE — 49

GETTING STARTED WITH TABLES — 49

RESIZING TABLE	50
MOVING TABLE	51
FORMATTING YOUR TABLES	51
ADDING A COLUMN	52
INSERTING A ROW	53
RESIZING ROWS & COLUMNS	55
MERGE CELLS	55
ALIGN CELL TEXT	56
ADDING CELL BORDER	58
CHANGING CELL COLOR	59
TEXT DIRECTION	61

CHAPTER FOUR — 62

OPERATING GRAPHICS — 62

Including images	62
Image Out of Google	64
Inserting clipart	66
Including Effects on Images	68
Insert a Caption	70
Cropping Images	71
Cropping to form	73
Readjusting Your Images	75
Wrapping Text around images	77
The Wrap points	78
Inserting Shapes To Your Publication	80
Changing Shapes	81
Altering The Color	82
Altering The Border	82
Including a Shadow	83
Adding Objects Alignment	85
The Objects Distribution	86
Objects Grouping Object	86
Setting Object Layers	88
The Page parts	89
Including Borders and Accents	93
Adding Calendars to Your Publisher	93
Inserting WordArt	97

CHAPTER FIVE — 103

PRODUCING MAIL MERGE — 103

Producing Mail Marge Envelopes	103
Producing Mail Merge Invitation	109
Making Use of Pre-designed Templates	113
Discovering a Pre-designed Template	114
Producing Your Template	116

CHAPTER SIX 118

OPERATING PUBLICATION 118

- Storing your Publication in a Different Format — 119
- How To Open Saved Documents — 122
- Page Setup — 124
- Producing Booklets — 126
- Making Use of Page Masters — 128
- Modifying Master Pages — 128
- Producing Master Pages — 131
- Using Master — 132
- Putting In Guides — 132

CHAPTER SEVEN 136

HOW TO PUBLISH YOUR WORK 136

- How To Print Your Documents — 136
- Printing As a Booklet — 138
- Exporting Your Work as a PDF — 141
- Sharing Of File — 142

CONCLUSION 144

INDEX 145

INTRODUCTION

Microsoft Publisher is one of the Microsoft Office suites structured to assist users in producing diverse sets of publications such as flyers, brochures, greeting cards, business cards, calendars, certificates, etc.

Microsoft Publisher is created in an easy format that anyone can make use of to produce an amazing publication. You can produce a publisher from the blank page by developing the publication from the beginning or premade templates.

Microsoft Publisher provides diverse benefits that you may never come across before unless you're being informed by someone else or you know how to operate Microsoft Publisher tools. You may never know how to optimize and bring out the best out of Microsoft Publisher if you don't have enough understanding to operate its tools which is the purpose for the creation of this "Step by Step User Guide for producing and structuring all types of publications".

I suggest this practical user guide for you as it entails the basic understanding you will require for operating Microsoft Publisher.

Chapter One
Beginning with Microsoft Publisher

With a publisher, you can easily create many diverse types of publications. Publisher differs from Microsoft Word in that exceptional significance is laid down on page layout design rather than text composition and attestability.

Microsoft Publisher is a desktop publishing Application developed by Microsoft. The publisher is analyzed as an entry-level desktop publishing application and is focused on home users, schools, and small businesses with in-house printing. Publisher is not used for commercial printing purposes.

The publisher uses a WYSIWYG interface (what you see is what you get), which simply means, that every single thing you create on the screen appears the same way when printed.

Publisher gives several qualities and tools to produce and polish publications such as posters, banners, flyers, letterheads, greeting cards, and banners. These tools are grouped into tabs in a menu system on the crest of the screen called a ribbon.

Publishers allow you to freely outline your designs on the page using objects such as text boxes for headings and body text, and image placeholders for photographs and shapes.

The publisher also involves building blocks for generating bigger publications named "page part" and pre-designed templates.

proofing tools such as grammar check, and spell checkers allow you to confirm your work as you type. Grammar errors are marked in green while the misspelled words are underlined in red. Frequently misspelled phrases or words are rectified by auto-correct features.

Act by the instructions listed below to start Microsoft Publisher on your PC:

1. Enter "**Publisher**" into the **Search** box at the base left of the Window
2. Then click the **'Publisher'** desktop app as a little shaded below.

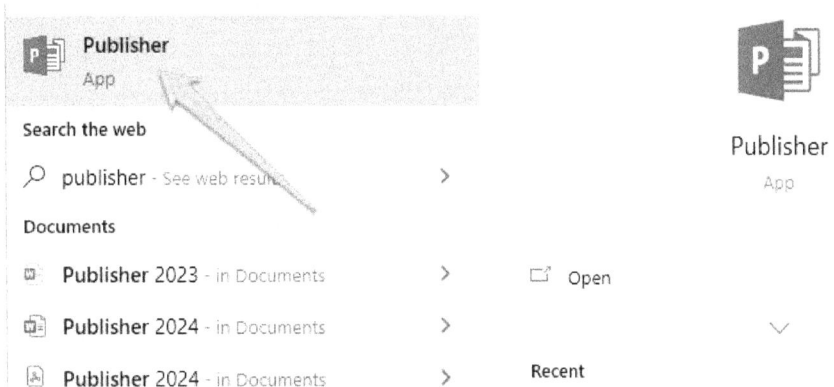

3. (Alternatively), click the **Start** button and click **Publisher** on the available items.

Creating a Shortcut for Publisher

To make it easy, you can pin the publisher icon on the taskbar. I discover this element handy. To do this keep to the steps beneath.

1. Right-click on the **Publisher** icon on the taskbar.
2. click "**pin to taskbar**".

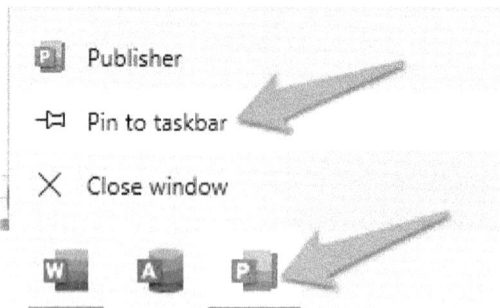

In this way, the publisher will on every occasion be on the taskbar anytime you require it.

Once the publisher starts, on the right-hand side you can pick a template from the thumbnails by clicking anyone to begin with.

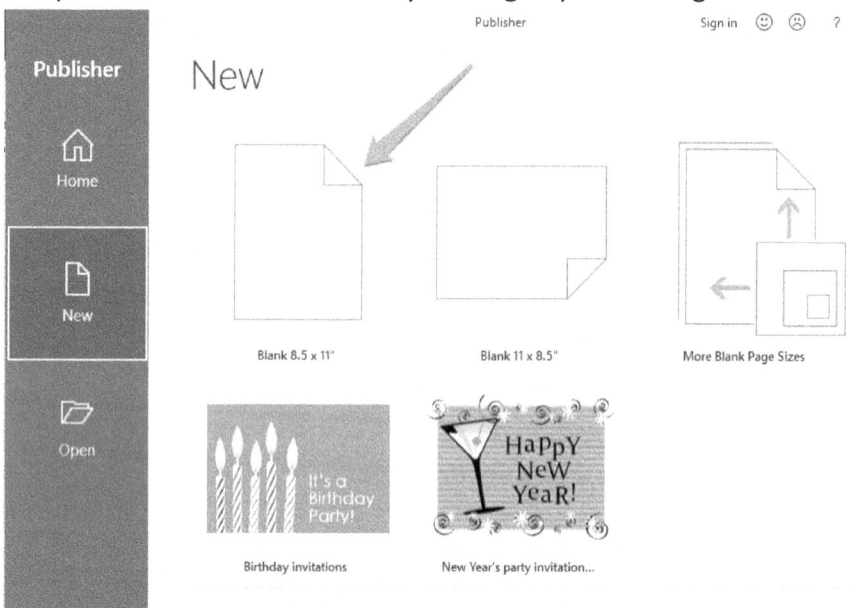

At the left-hand side green pane your most newly saved publications will be displayed, let's concisely take a view at the publisher's main screen. Here we can see beneath, the screen is broken into divisions

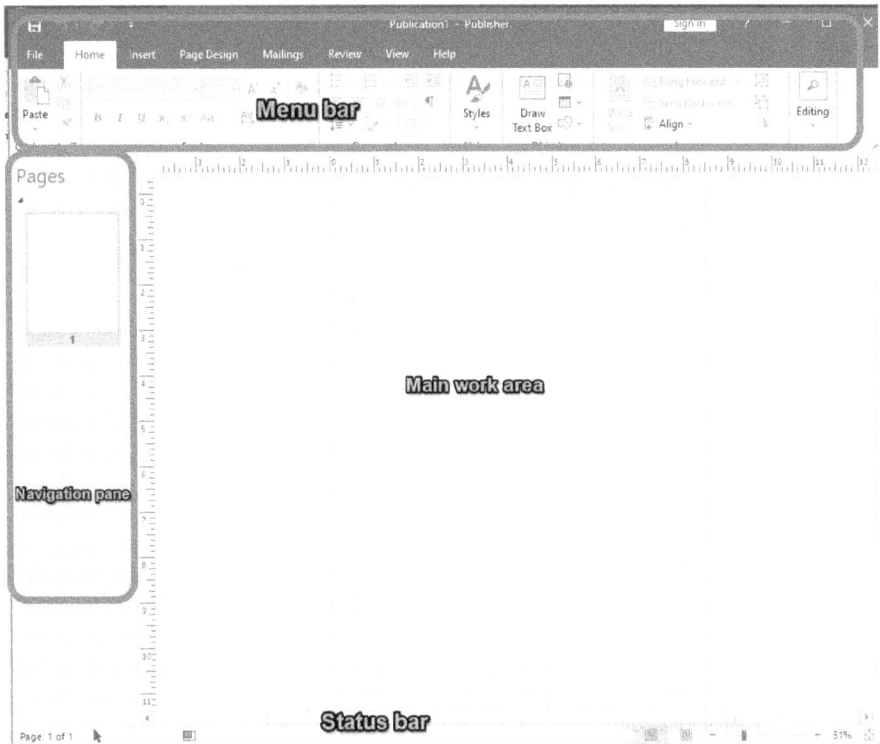

Ribbon Tabs

Publisher tools are grouped into tabs called ribbons along the top of the screen, tools are classified according to their use, and they are as follows.

The Home Tab

All tools that as to do with test generating, such as: interchanging the fonts and making text bold, and the most familiar tools for alignment and text formatting.

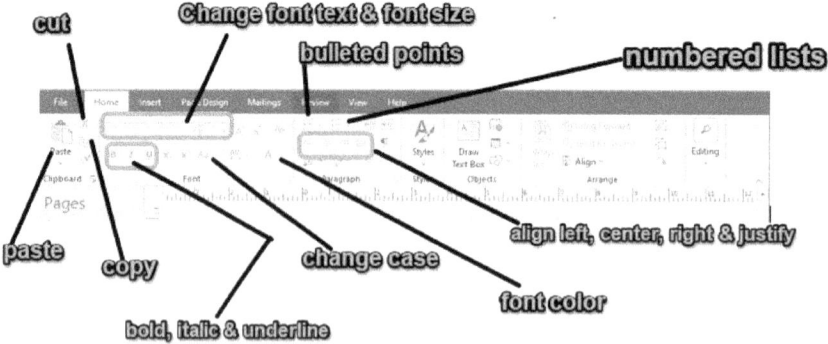

The Insert Tab

All tools that as to do with putting charts, tables, borders, graphics images, etc.

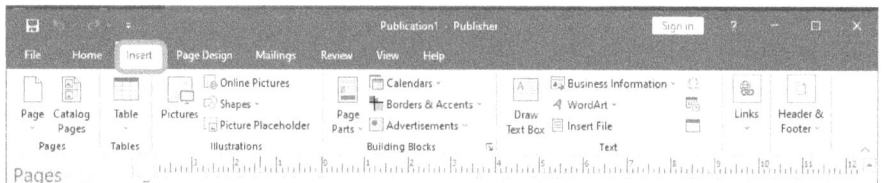

You can also put graphics, equations, word Art, page parts, pre-designed ads, page parts, and smart art using the "building blocks" and "illustrations" sections of the ribbon.

You can also involve or put word art, text boxes, and symbols using the text section of the ribbon.

Page Design Tab

The page design ribbon allows you to modify the margin, page orientation, and size, switch templates, and establish design guides to assist you with the components on your page.

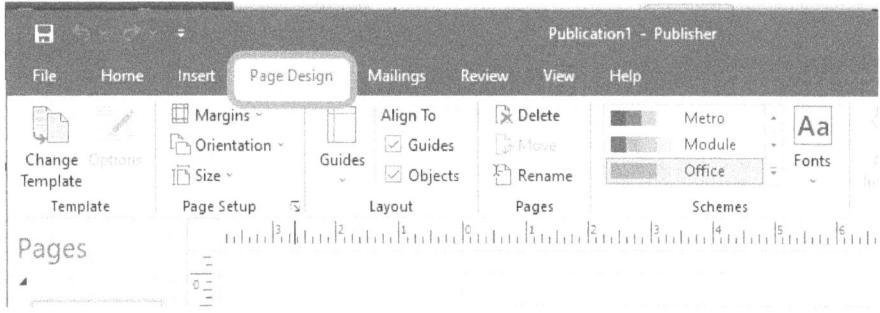

You can also put up page masters, interchange the background, and select or elect pre-designed schemes.

The Mailing Tab

Mailing ribbon allows you to initiate mail merges in your publisher document and link it to a data source in a spreadsheet

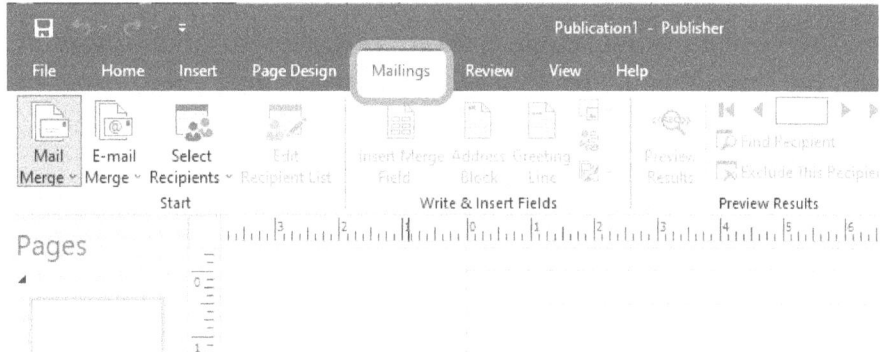

The Review Tab

You can do some analysis with the review ribbon, and you can also spell-check your document, translate text into other languages, and lock up words in the thesaurus.

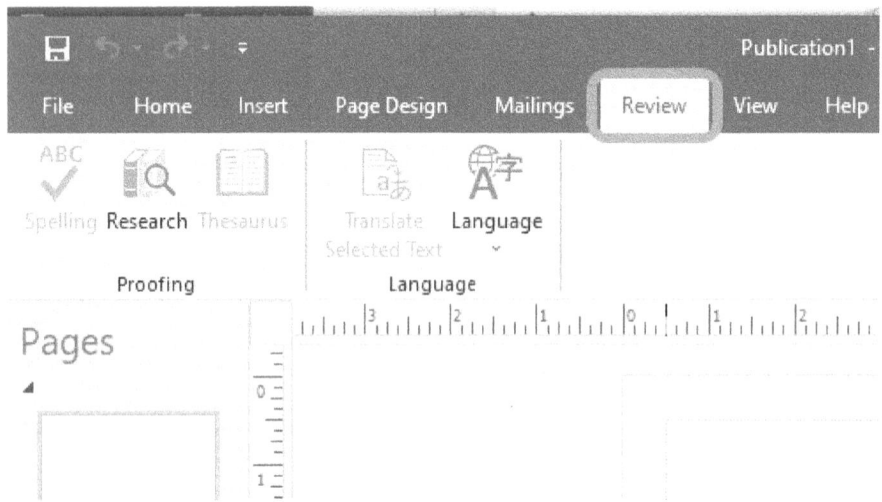

The View Tab

You can switch the default view, attach rulers, zoom, and navigation with the view ribbon, and also interchange your open master pages by using the view ribbon.

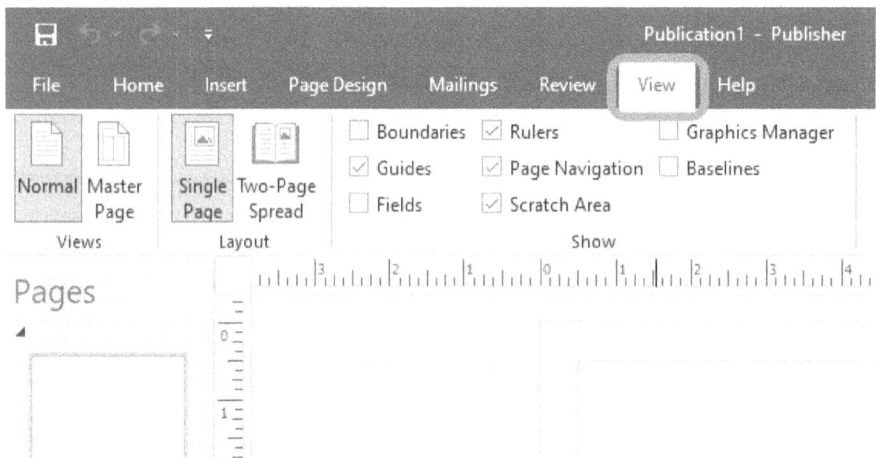

The File Backstage

When you click "File" on the topmost of your screen on the left-hand side, this will unfold what Microsoft relates to as the "Backstage".

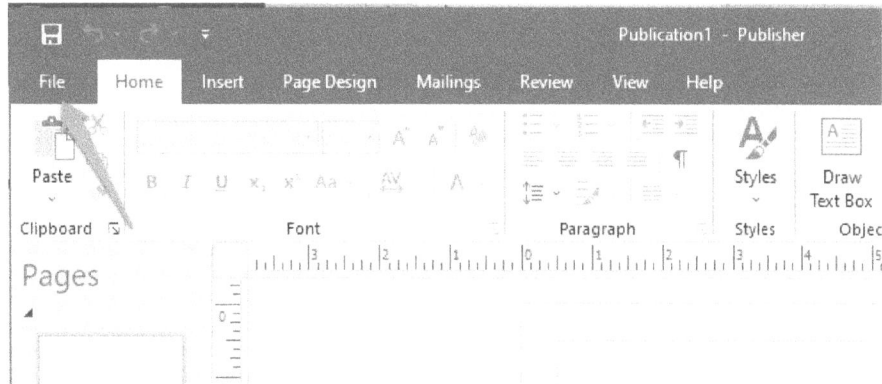

Backstage is where you save or open publications, export or share publications, print, as well as options, preference settings, and a Microsoft account.

You can also interchange publication preferences, and Microsoft Account Settings, login, and commence your Microsoft Office.

Building A New Design

You can smoothly make numerous designs with Microsoft Publisher, you can sketch them from scrape, or one of the many distinct patterns or frameworks involved with the application.

Chapter Two
Commencing with a New Publication

There will be a need for a minute option concerning a definite feature, such as page layout, paper type, and size before you make a new publication. Some of the choices you have to make about your publication include page layout. Making a publication from a template takes care of most of the following for you.

Size Of The Publication

Some publications, like flyers, can be minute A5 or A6. Other publications comprise such posters that are a lot larger, A1 or A3.

About Orientation

Landscape or Portrait. Several flyers are portrait, as well as most posters. Greetings cards can also be both landscape and portrait orientation.

About Margins

The sectors of blank space around the peak, base, right, and left side of a printed publication are called **"margins"**.

Unlock a new publication

You will be able to choose a template, to start with, or produce a blank publication when you unlock Publishers. For this demo choose "blank A4 (portrait)".

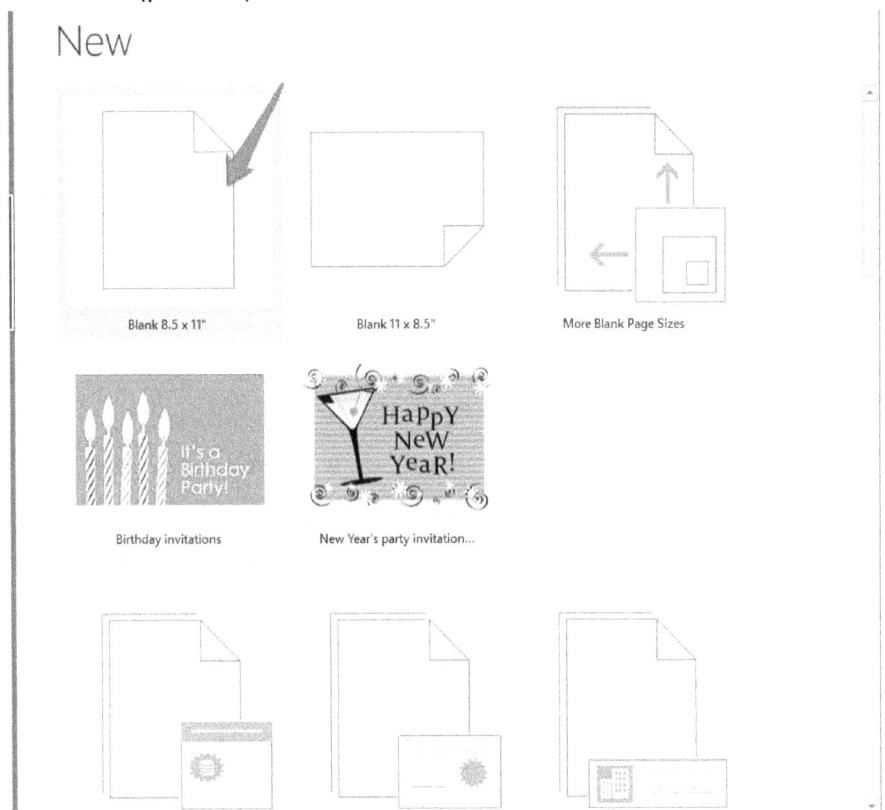

If you are operating your publisher currently, tick "File" on the topmost screen at the left-hand side then choose "New". You will land on the publisher's main work area, and instantly you will pick a New template.

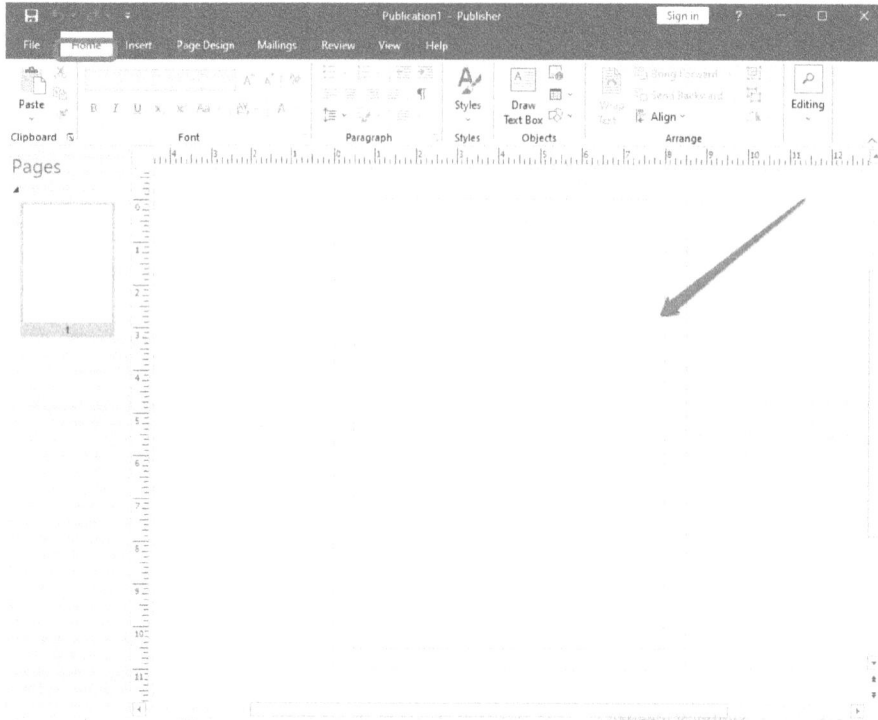

Now we can start producing our publication.

Major Workspace

Soon your page navigation pane is on the left-hand side. Now, you can find the page number in your navigation pane. There is a need for you to tick on the page thumbnails in the navigation pane to get to that page.

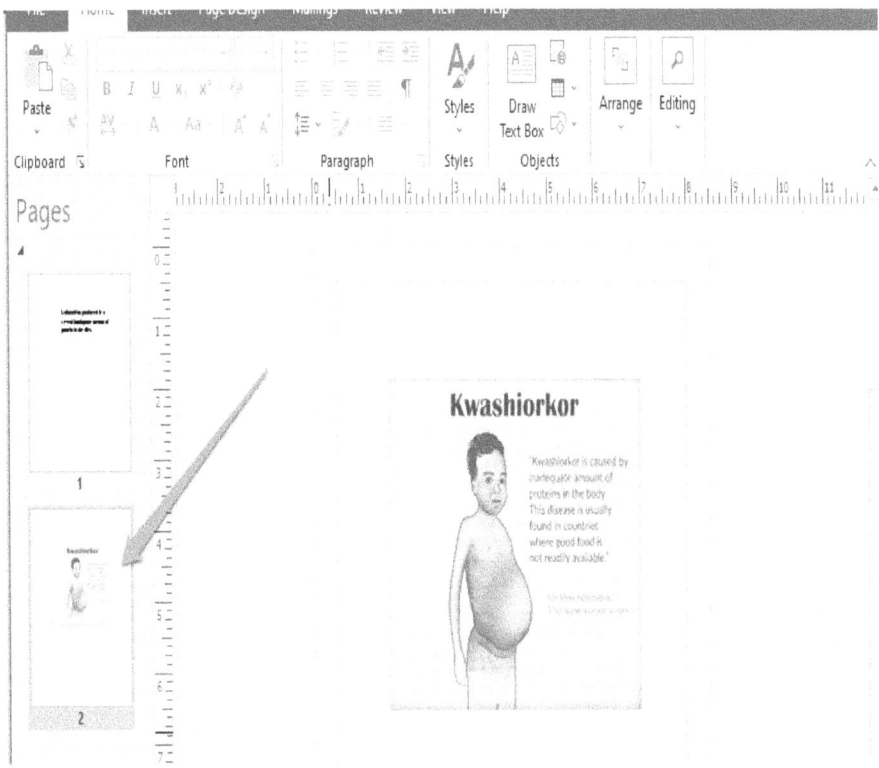

You will find three sets of values at the bottom (the underside) of the screen. The foremost will show the page number you are present, tick to unfold, and close the page navigation pane. The next set will let you know the position of the peak and left edges of an object on your page. And so the object picked beneath is 12.75cm down from the right and 4.92cm from the left corner of the page. The final set of numbers will show the size of the picked object.

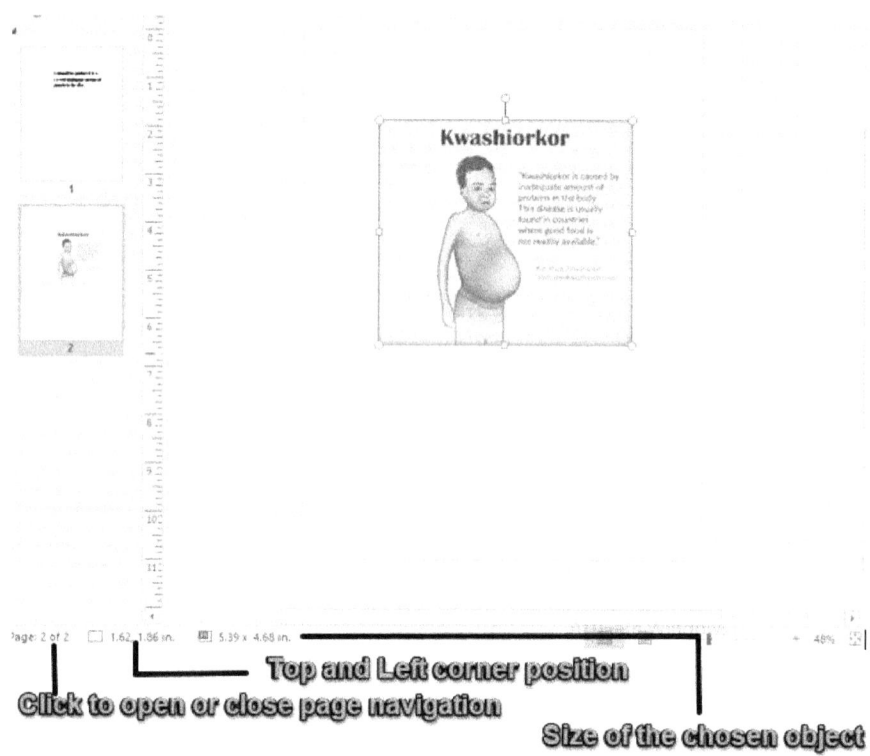

On the downright, you will observe the page zoom and page view controls

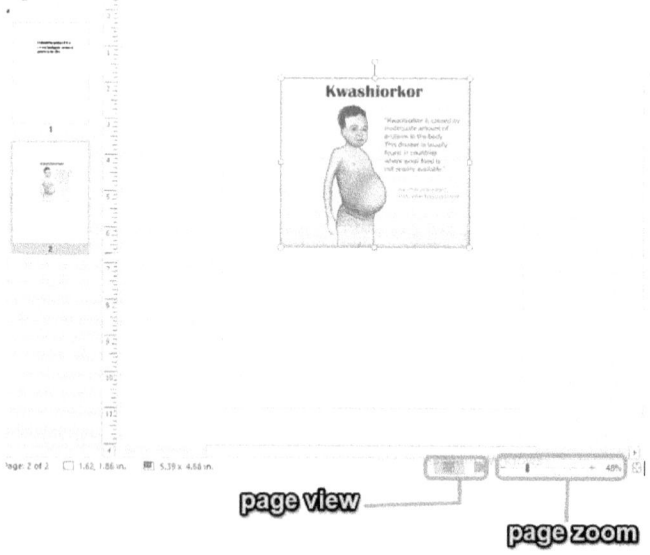

HOW TO WORK WITH GUIDES

To produce guidelines that will help you to fix the components on your design, tick either the vertical or horizontal ruler, then you can drag the mouse pointer to the position on your page.

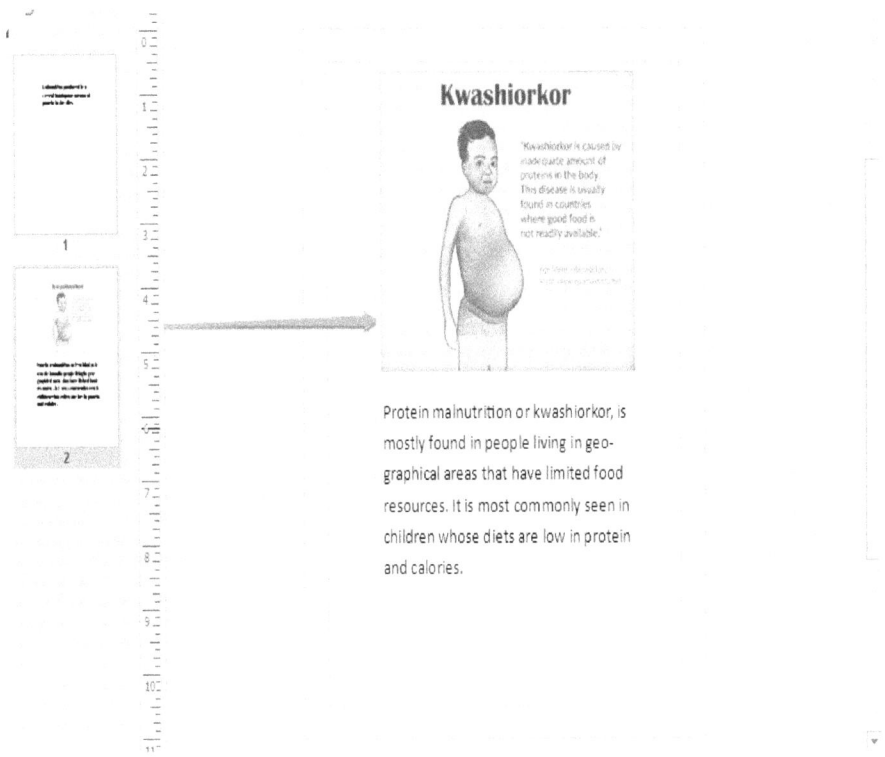

The Basic Element

Publisher documents are sketched using some of these basic elements such as image placeholder and image placeholder.

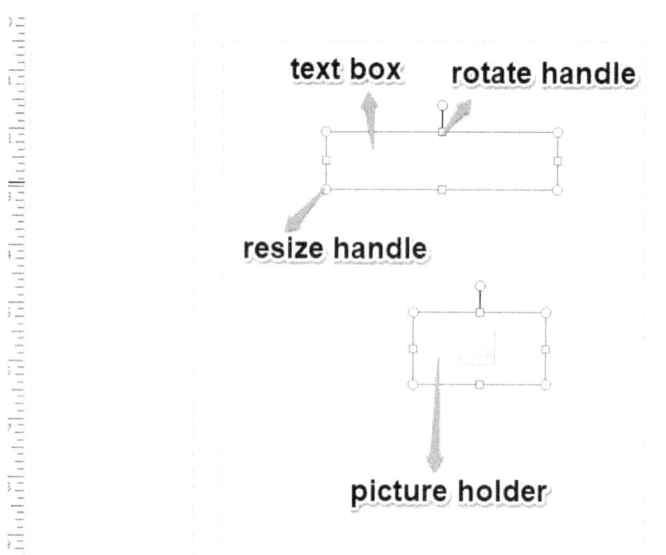

You can attach text boxes to your design to require the text and position it singly. You can repeat it with image placeholders. These are used to position images in your design. These can also be referred to as placeholders" Frames". When you tick on a placeholder or frame, small circles will show around the corner and they are referred to as handles. You can tick and drag on the handles to resize your image placeholder or text box, you can also attach tables, charts, and shapes to your designs.

Addition of a Text Box

To attach some text to your design, firstly attach a text box, and for you to attach a text box, go to the home ribbon
And choose "draw text box".

Tick and drag the text box on your page

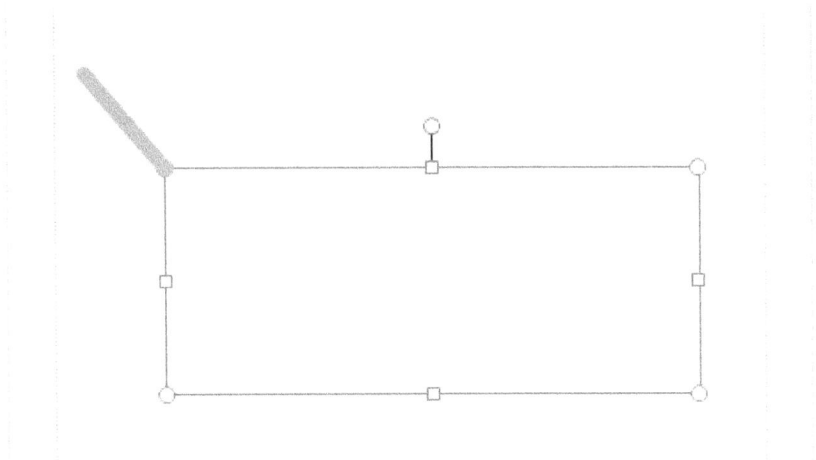

How To Create Text

You can type in some text, once you have pressed the text box.

Learning How To Format Text

You can format your text inside your text box by employing the basic formatting tools on the home ribbon.

Font Specifying

Heed to these steps to interchange the font

1. Highlight the text you want to interchange.

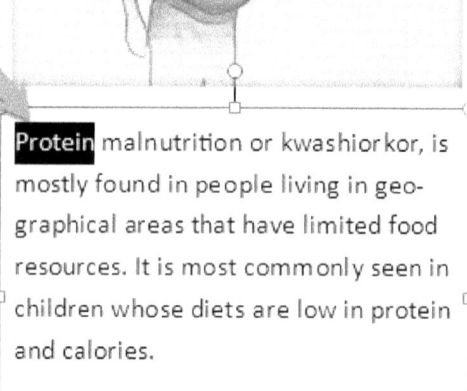

2. Click on the font from the home ribbon, then pick the font you want, from the drop-down box.

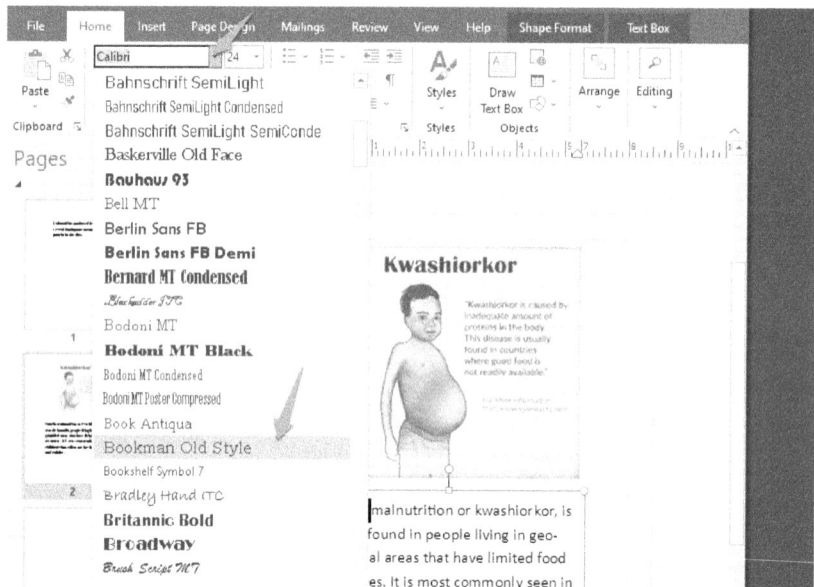

Font Size Adjustment

The text you want to change requires to be highlighted.

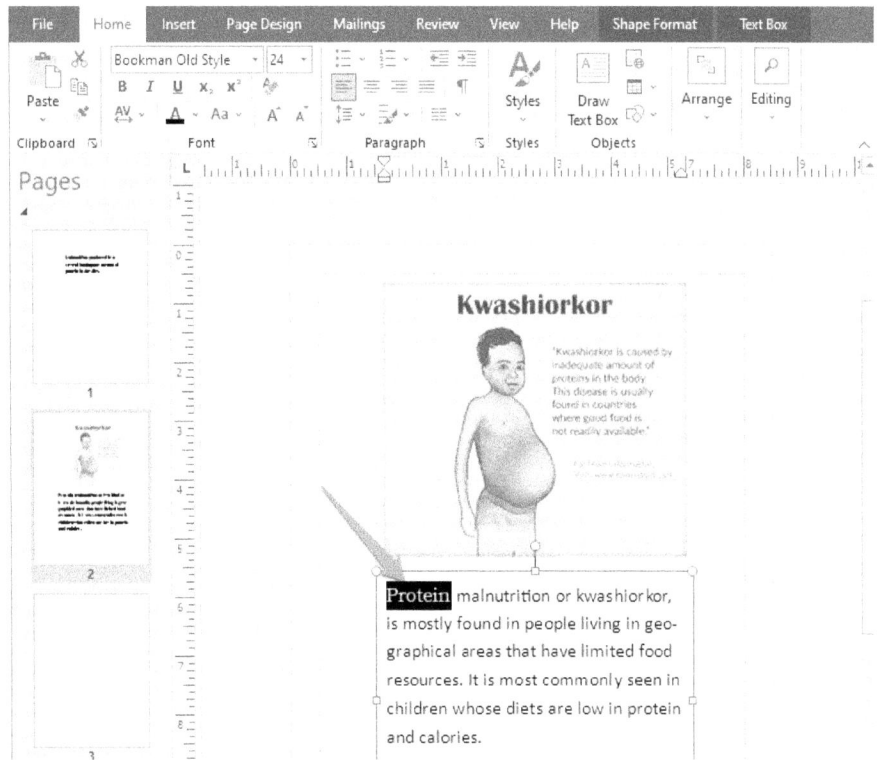

Choose the font size from the home ribbon, then from the drop-down pick the size you want.

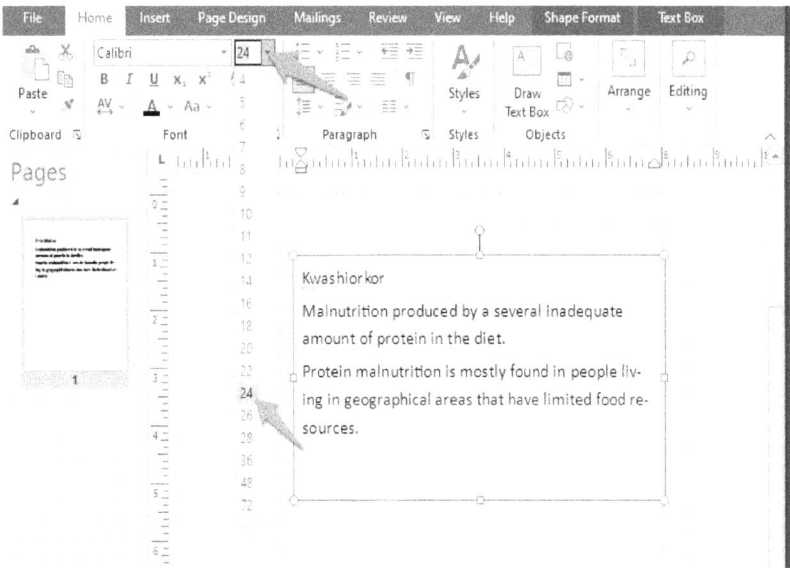

Bold, italic, underlined

Highlight the text you need to interchange.

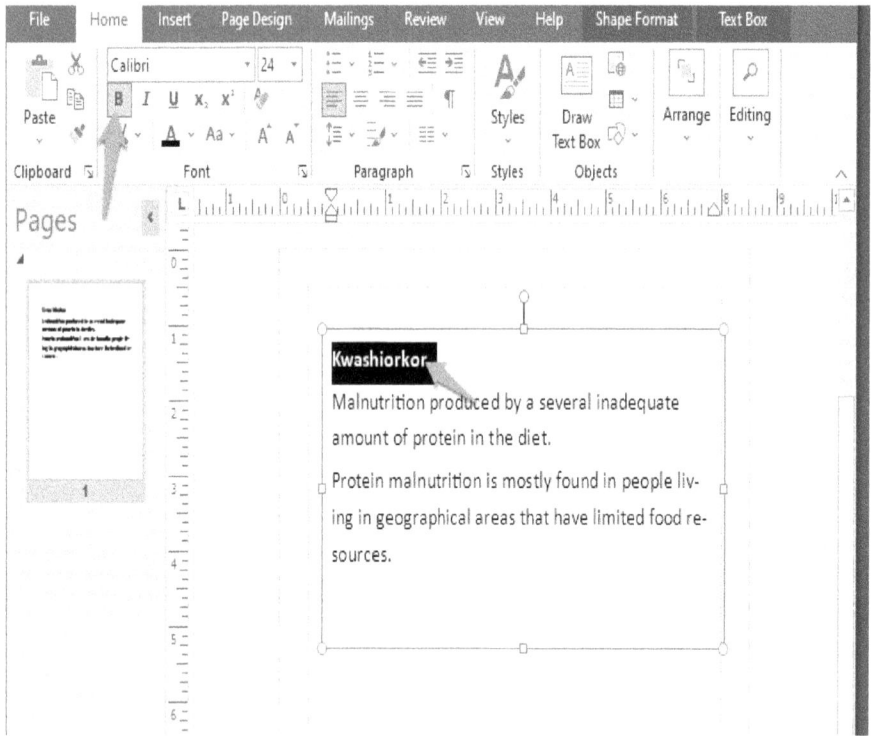

Click the bold icon on the topmost left of the home ribbon. You can also do likewise for Italic and underlined text.

Alternating The Text Color

Highlight the text that you want to change.

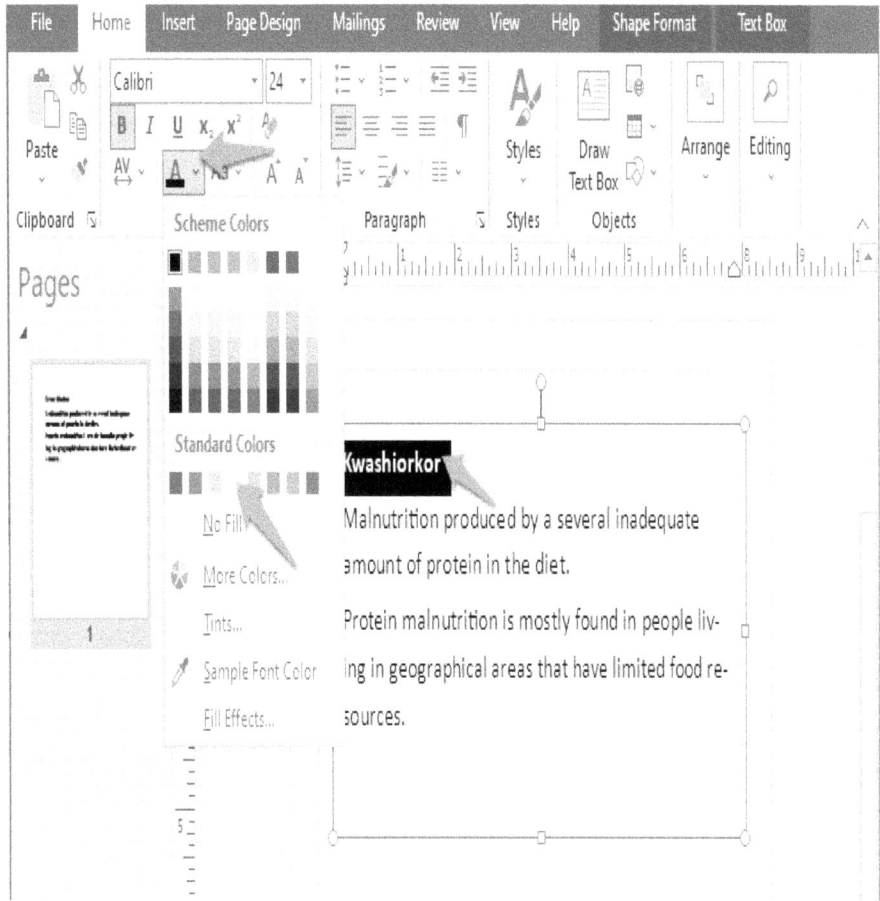

Choose the font color icon from the home ribbon. Pick a color from the drop-down options.

Specification of Text Alignment

In the inner of your text box, text can be aligned to the right, to the left, or the center. You can also justify text completely so that a text block is aligned to both the right and left of the text box.

To accomplish this, choose the text you want to align.

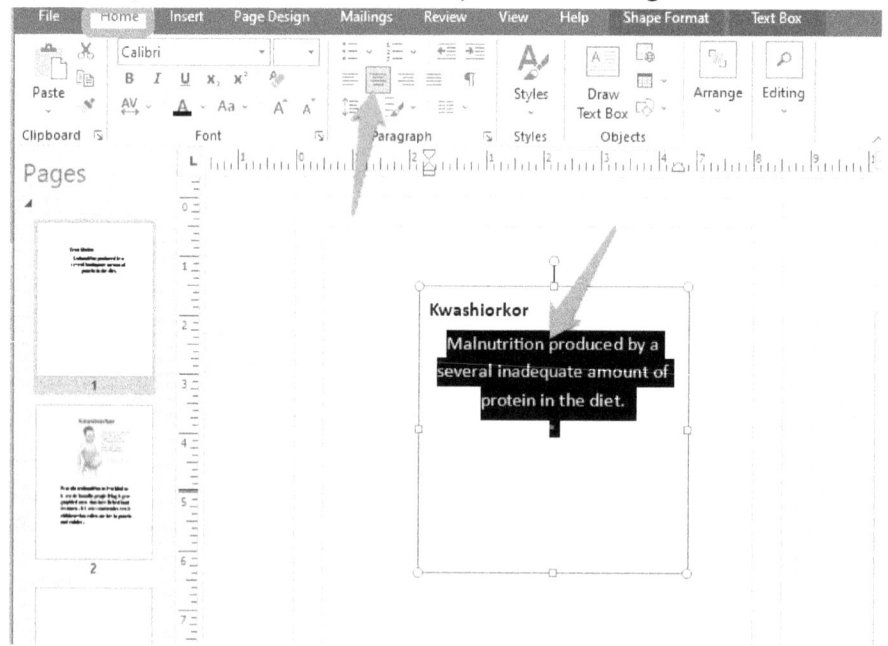

Then choose a paragraph alignment icon, from the home ribbon.

Changing Of the Case

You can swiftly change the case of the text to UPPERCASE, lowercase, or sentence case. To produce this, choose your text.

Single out the case change icon from the home tab.

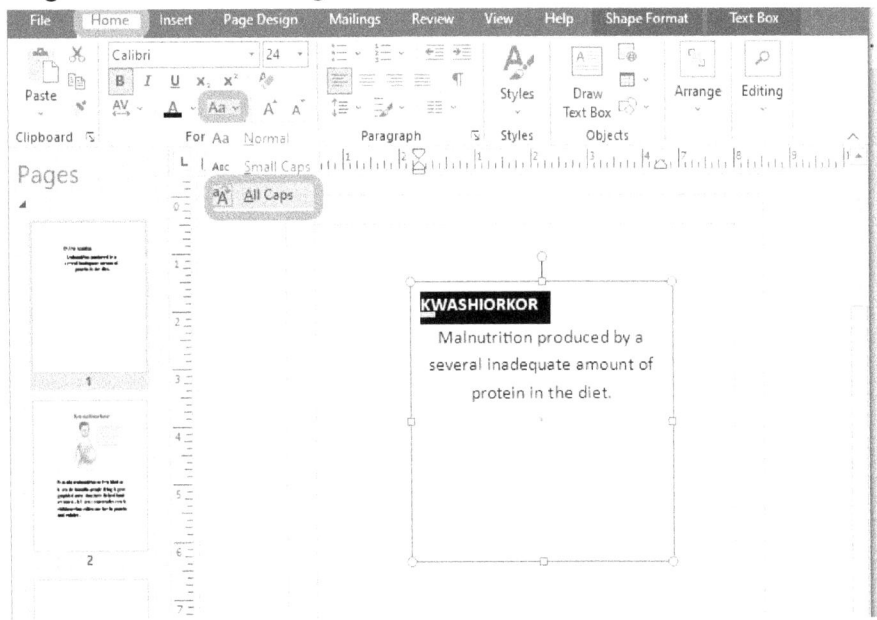

Scanning Typography Properties

The publisher comprises different typography properties that would help you to format your text. It is necessary to take note that these effects only apply to some fonts, like Cambria, Salfino, Gabriola, and Garamond.

Including Drop Cap Properties

A drop cap enlarges the first letter of the selected text and is mostly used at the block of text or the beginning of the chapter. To accomplish this, you are required to click on the paragraph you want to drop the cap.

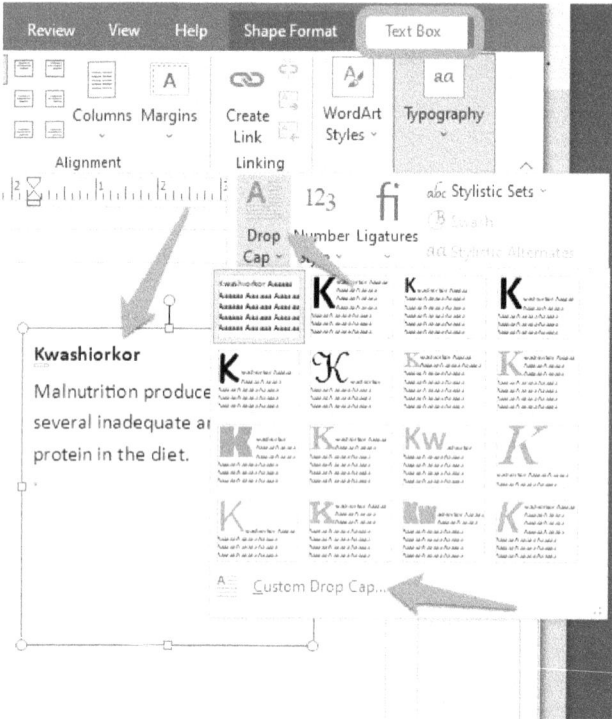

From the "text box tools" format ribbon, choose "drop cap" You can now click "custom drop cap" or choose a pre-set style from the choices.

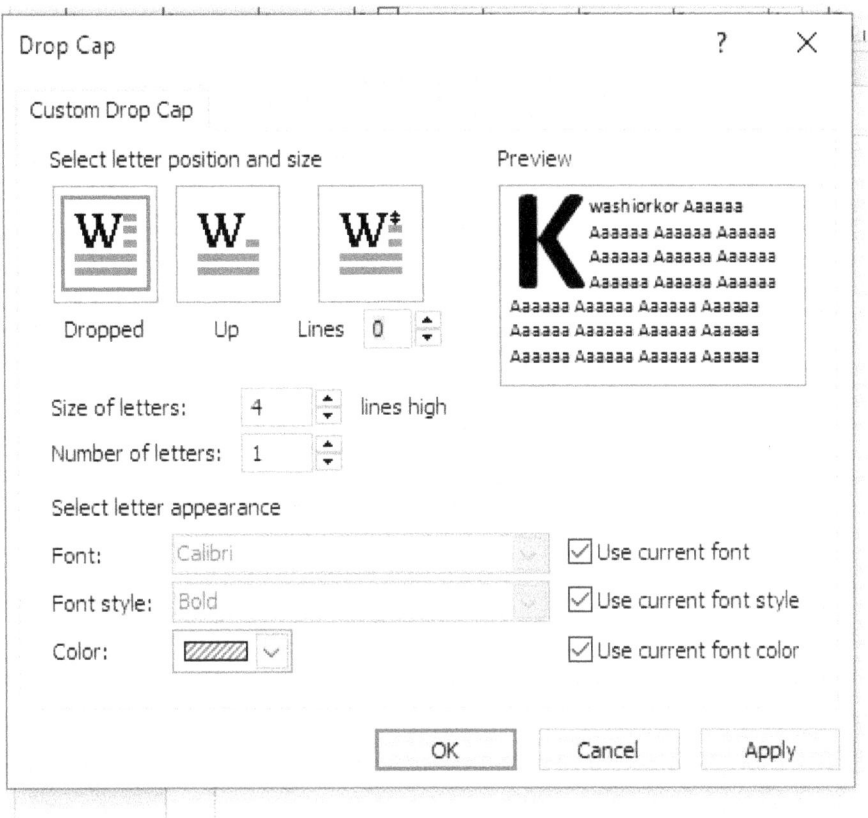

You can change the size of letters to occupy your drop cap into the paragraph, you can as well change the font and color. Tick 'apply' when you have completed it.

The Stylistic sets

These sets allow you to choose between different styles for your fonts, especially in the form of exaggerated serifs or flourishes. Also highlight the letter, from the 'text box tools' format ribbon chooses 'stylistic sets'

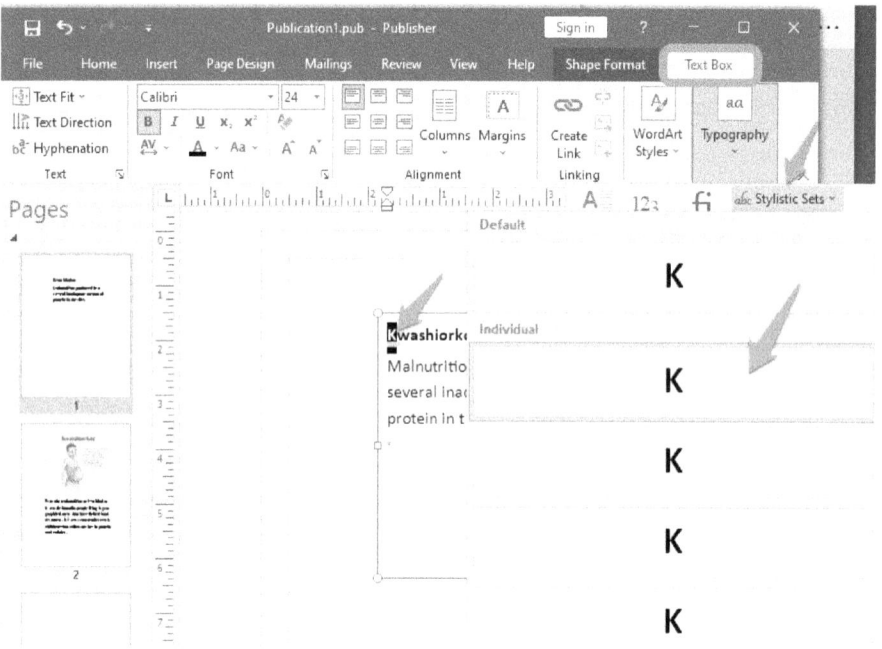

Now pin a choice from the drop-down box.

Simultaneously, utilize a stylistic set of words. It is also important for producing fancy headings and titles.

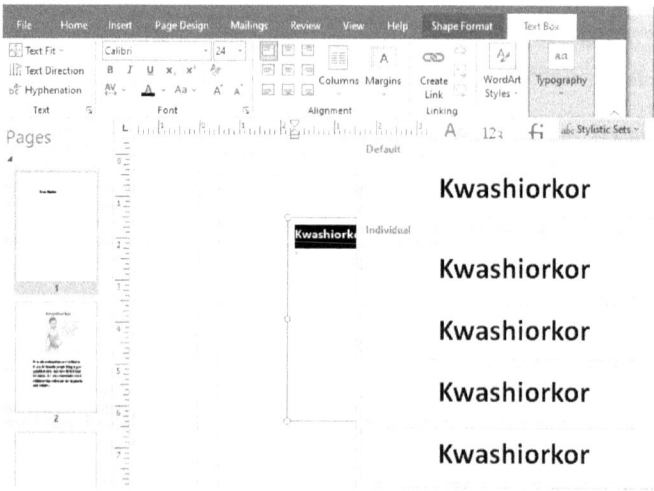

The Ligatures

Ligatures join definite combinations of letters to make them so easier to read. There are many different ligatures. *ff, ct, fi sp, st, ffi, th are* the most familiar.

The ligature can be turned on from the "text box tools" format ribbon. Choose the character, then pick "ligature".

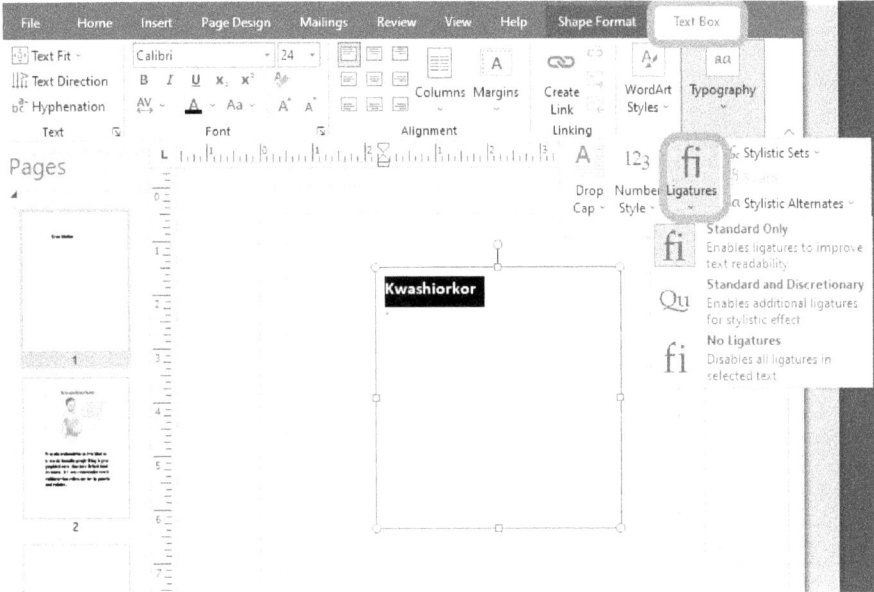

The Stylistic Alternatives Feature

This provides various versions of some letters. You will find these alternatives on the "text box tools" format ribbon. Choose the character, then pick "stylistic Alternative".

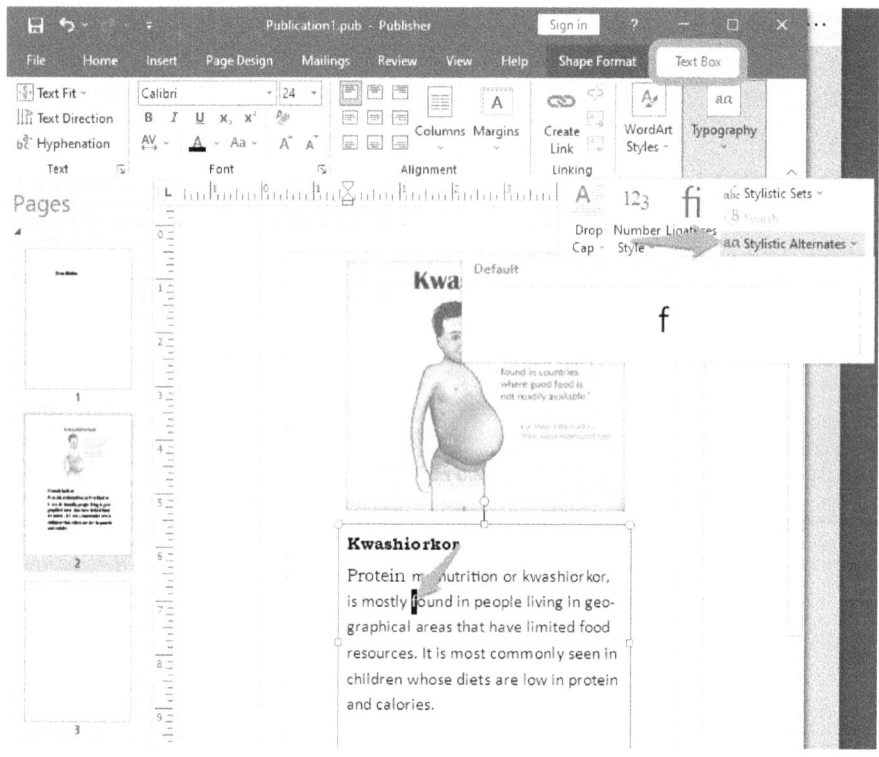

The Text Effects

You can add reflections, glow, bevel, and shadows to your text, also interchange the style, and add fill color and outline.

Shadow Feature

If you want to add a shadow, choose the text you want to use, from the 'text box tools' format tab, then pick 'text effects'.

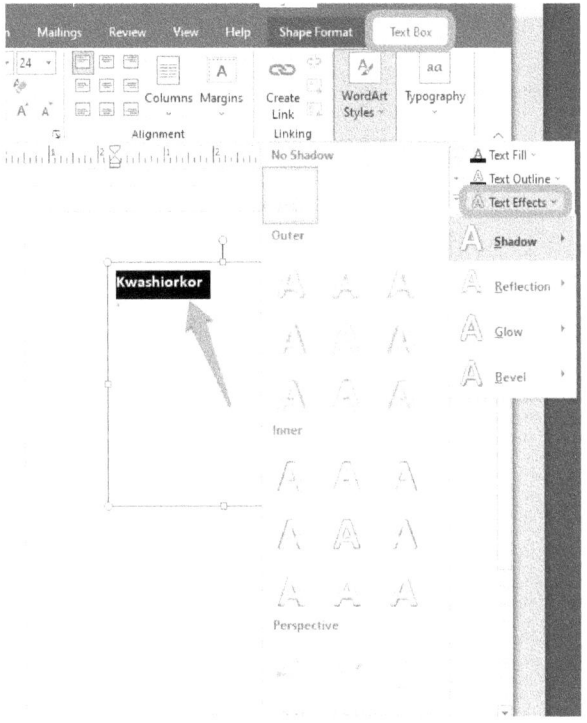

Choose an effect from the ones listed. You can also add a glow, reflection, or bevel effect from here.

Text Outline

To add an outline, you will have to select the text you want to use, then from the 'text tools' format tab, select 'text outline.'

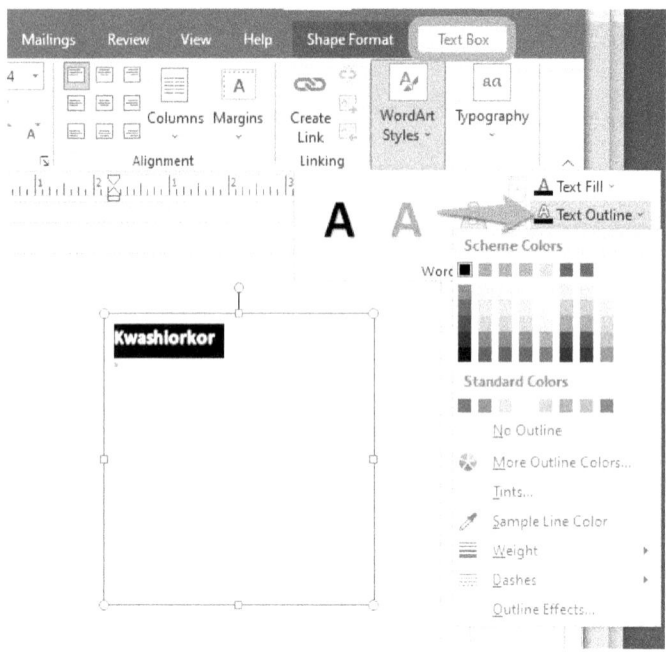

WordArt styles

To use Word art style, select the text you would like to use, then from the 'text box tools' format tab, select a style from the Word art.

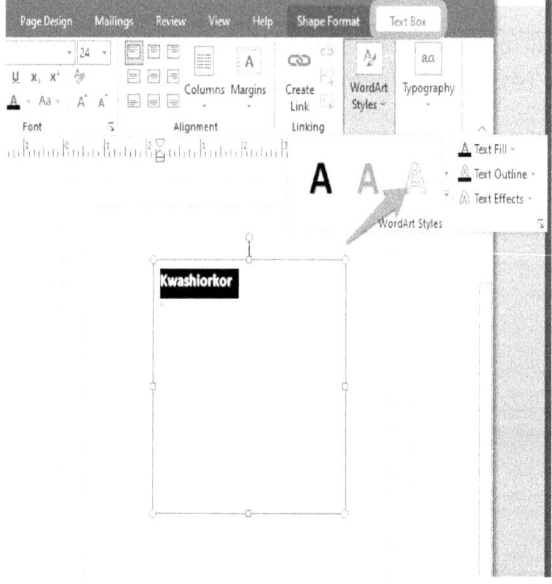

To look at more styles, tick the small down arrow near the WordArt styles.

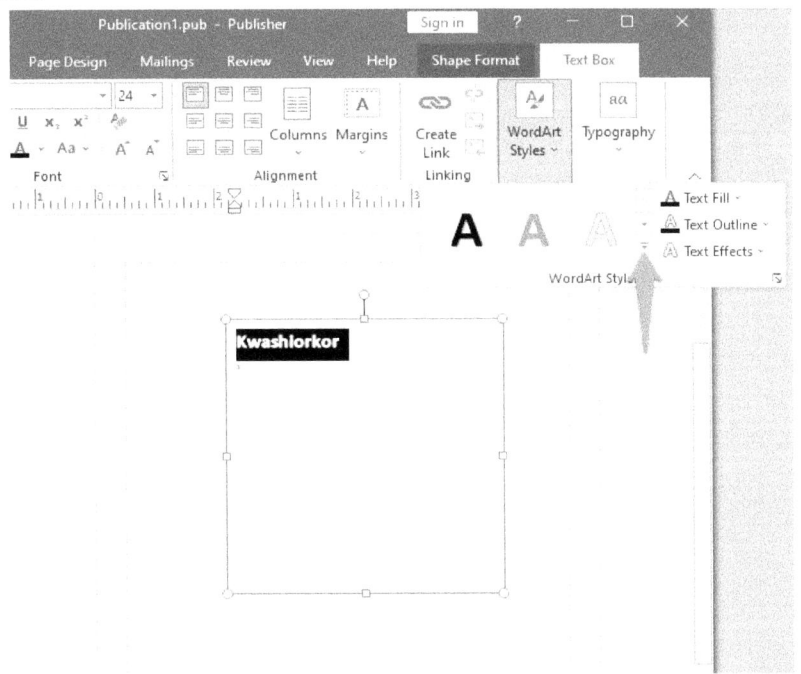

You will see a list of options.

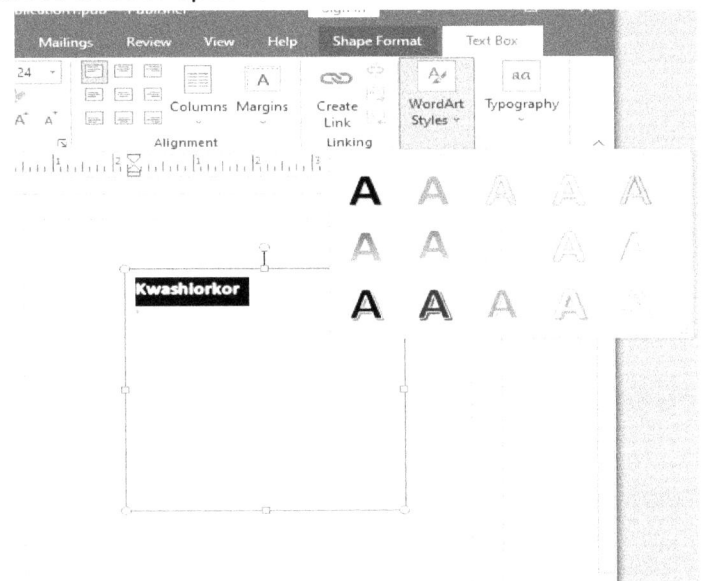

Select a style. You can select from many fixed styles.

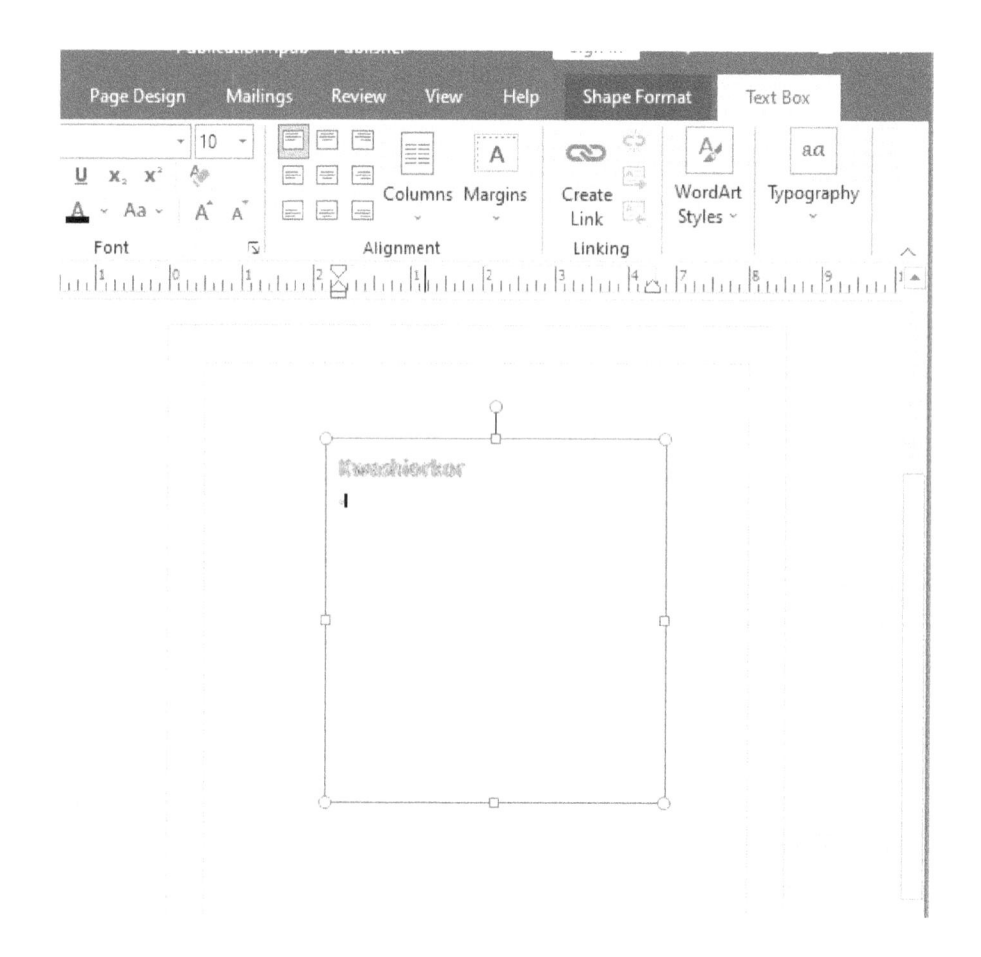

Text Boxes Formatting

You can involve reflections, bevels, and shadows in your text boxes, you can also put in another style, and also put an outline and fill color.

Background Color Change

Choose the text box and under the 'drawing tools' pick the 'format' ribbon. Choose 'shape fill'.

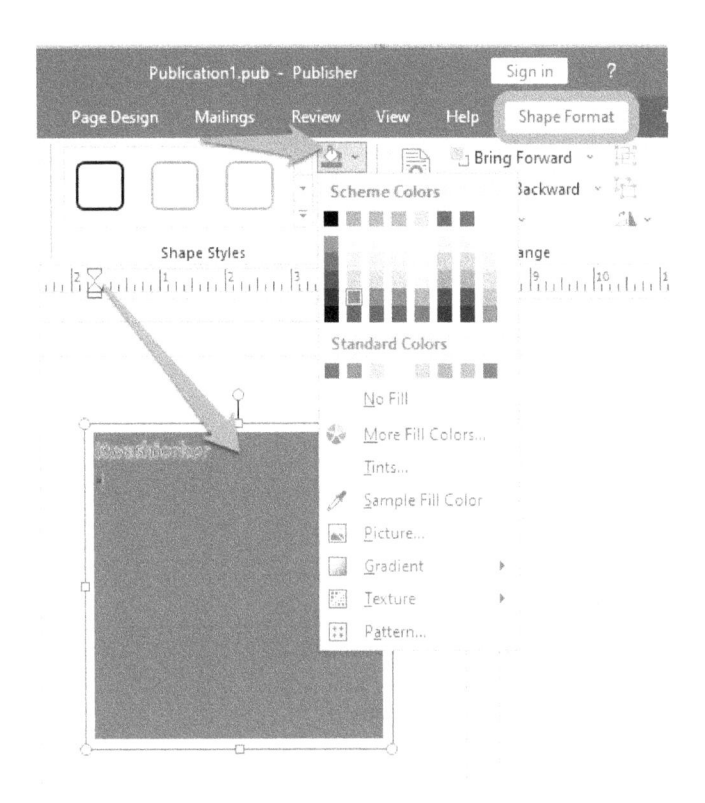

You can then choose a color from the drop-down options.

The Borders

Pick the text box, then beneath the 'drawing tools' choose the 'format' ribbon. Pick 'shape outline'.

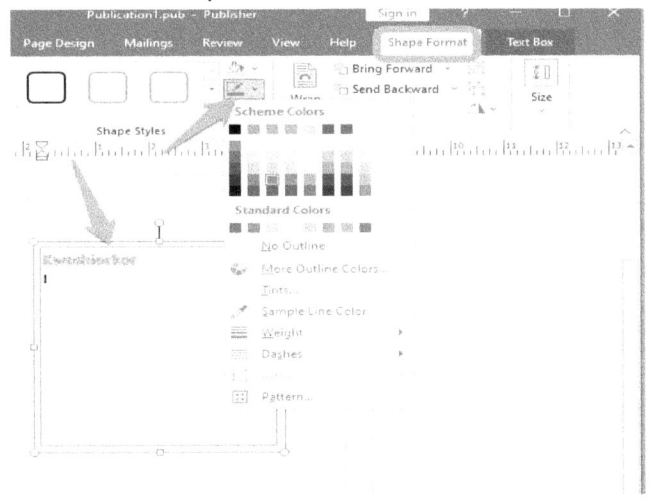

Pick any color from the drop-down options.

The Shadows

Choose the text box, beneath the 'drawing tools' pick the 'format' ribbon. Then pick the 'shape effects'.

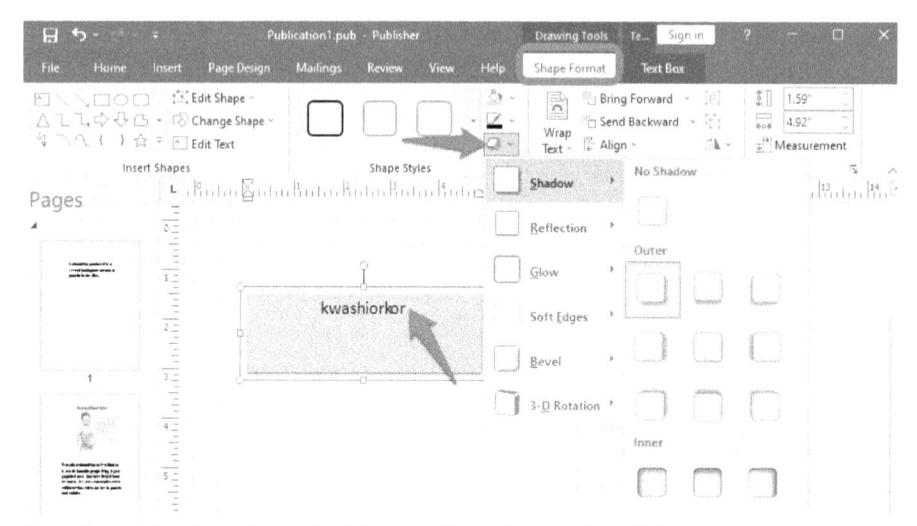

Scroll to 'shadows', and pick an effect from the slideout.

The Styles

There are different fixed styles you can use to make your text boxes beautiful. To employ them:

1) Choose the text box, and select the 'Drawing tool format' tab.
2) Tick the little arrow close to the shape styles to open the panel.

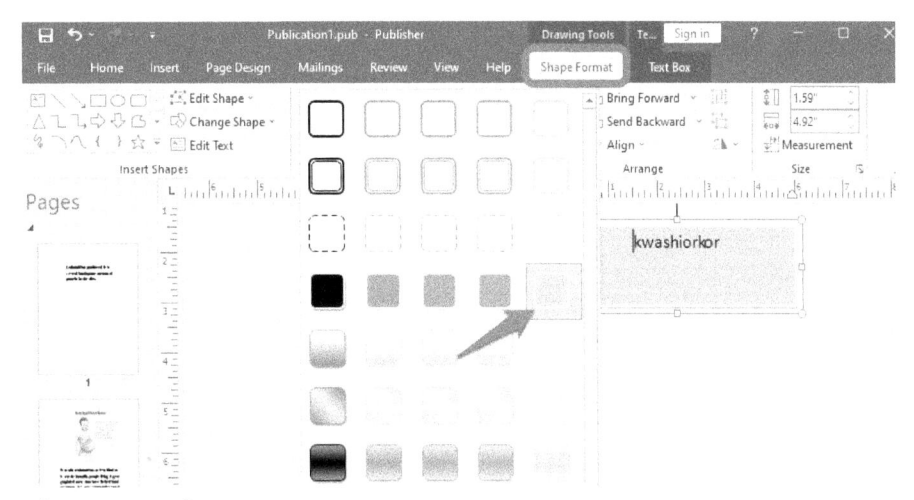

Choose a style.

Changing Text Boxes

You can change the size, move, and rotate the text boxes, you can also interchange the margins, alignment, and text direction.

Readjusting Text Box

Tick the text box's border to move a text box. Then drag the box to its recent location.

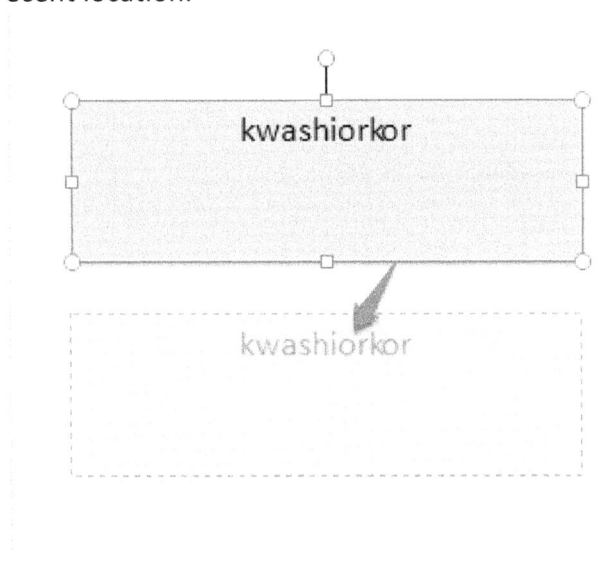

Resizing The Text Box

For you to reshape a text box, click and drag one out of the reshape handles till the box is the size you want.

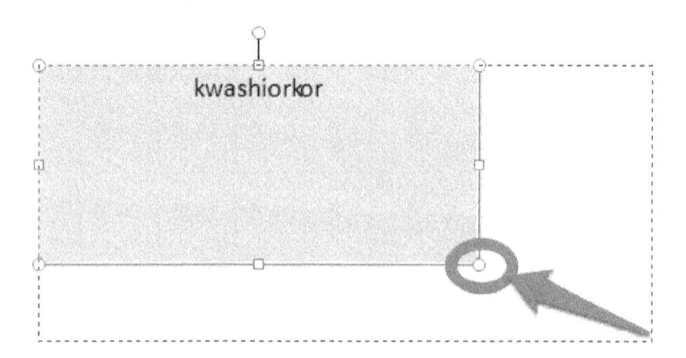

Rotation Of The Text Box

To rotate a text box, tick and drag the rotate handle on the crest central of the box. After that drag your mouse to the left or right to modify the rotation.

The Text Direction

The side of the text in a text box can be altered. To rotate your text, choose the text box, from the 'text box tools' format ribbon, and tick 'text direction'.

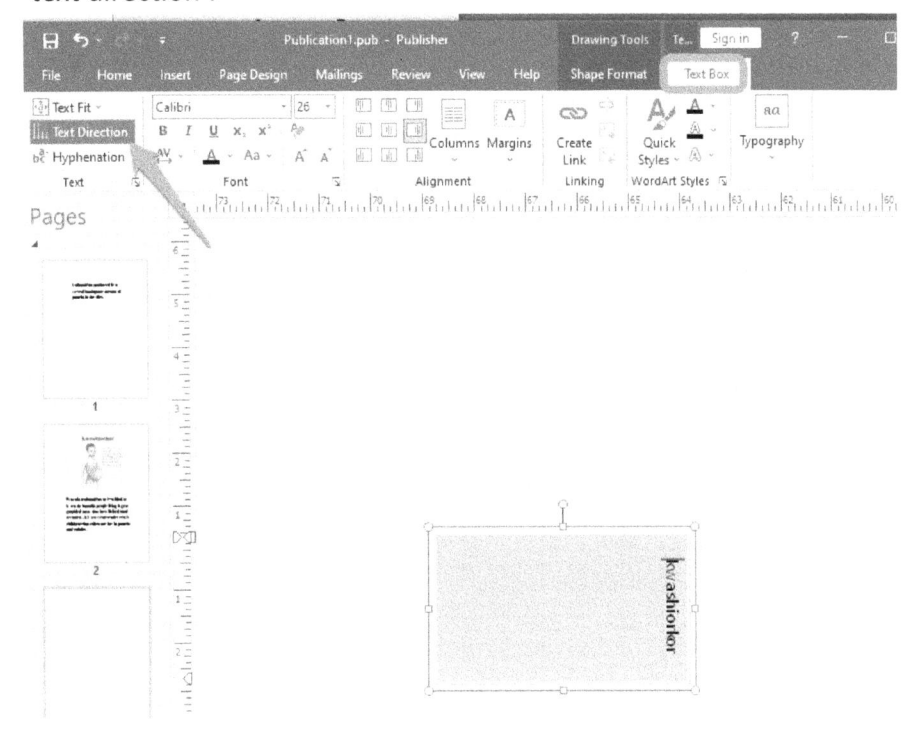

Text Autofit

You can of course sort and fit your text boxes. For you to do this, choose the text box you want to alter, then from the format tab under 'text box tools', pick 'text fit'.

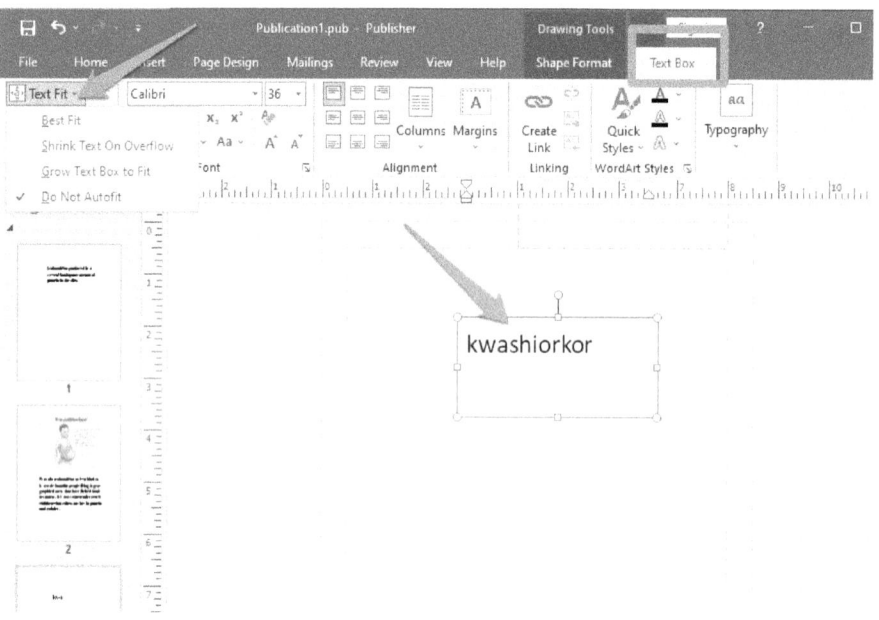

Choose a choice from the drop-down options. The best fit allows the text bigger or smaller to fit the text box.

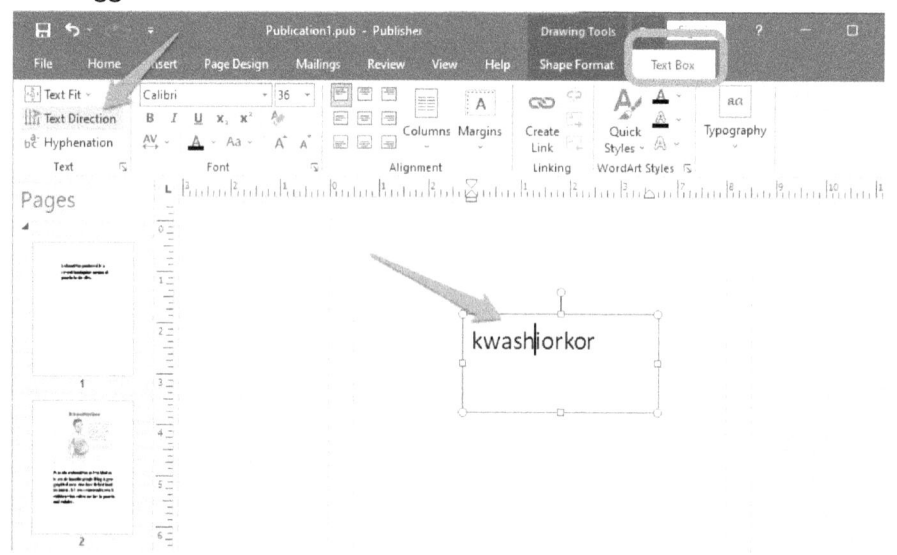

Lessening text on overflow naturally shrinks the text as you type to fill the size of the text box. Grow text box to fit naturally enlarges the size of the text box by the text's size.

The Text Box Margins

You can modify the margins in the text box. The margin is the gap between the text and the edge of the text box. Choose the text box, to modify the text margin.

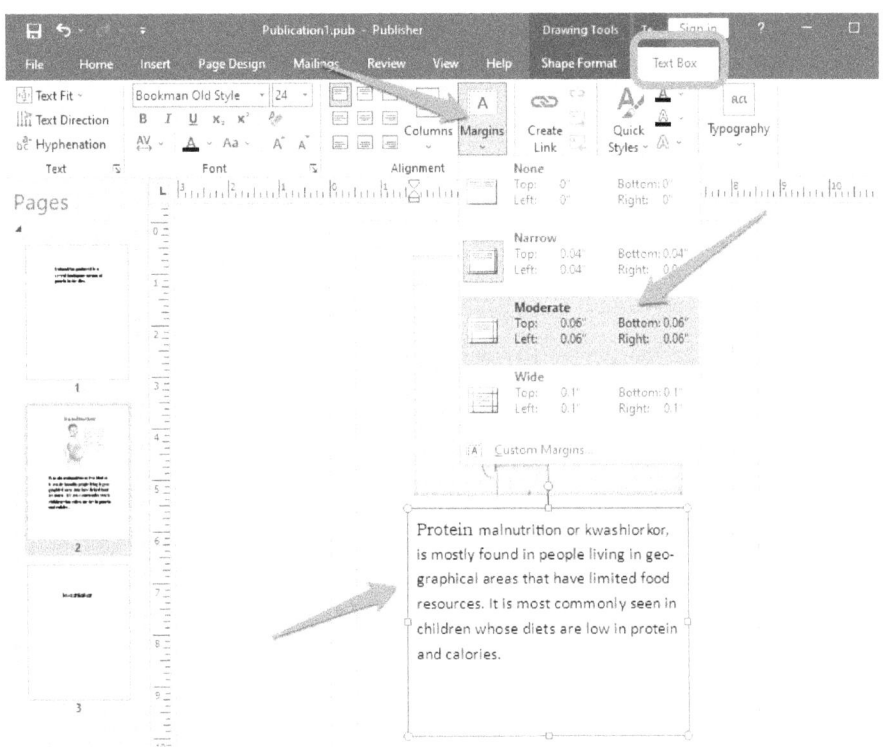

From the 'text box tools' format ribbon, choose 'margins'. You can also pick one out of the four presents, or click 'custom margins'.

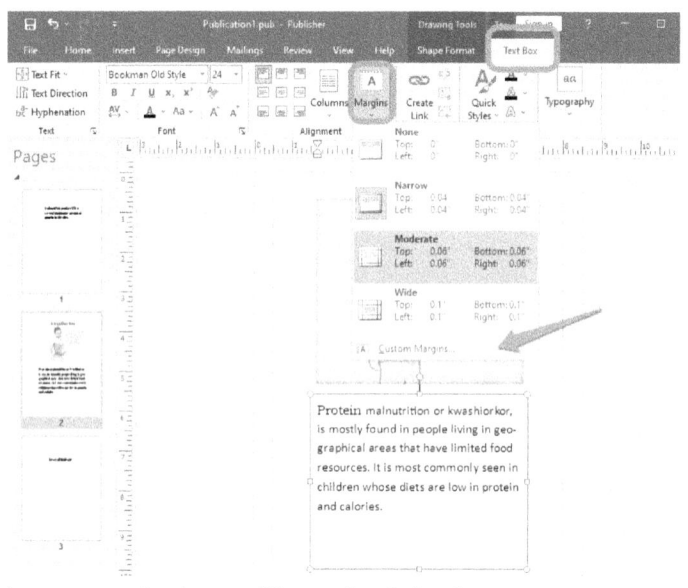

Forward, you can singly modify each of the four margins.

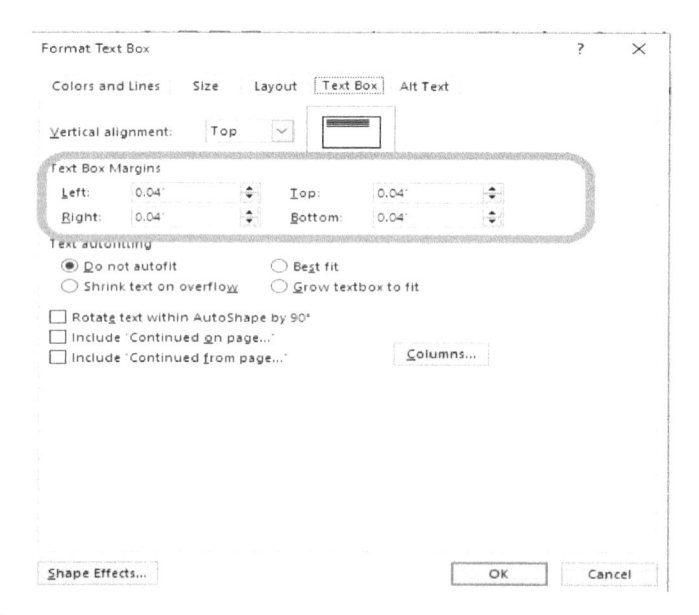

Aligning

Your text can be aligned inside your text box. You can also align to the top, bottom, right, left, or middle. For you to accomplish this, tick the text box, then from the 'text box tools' format ribbon, from the alignment section on the ribbon, choose the alignment icon.

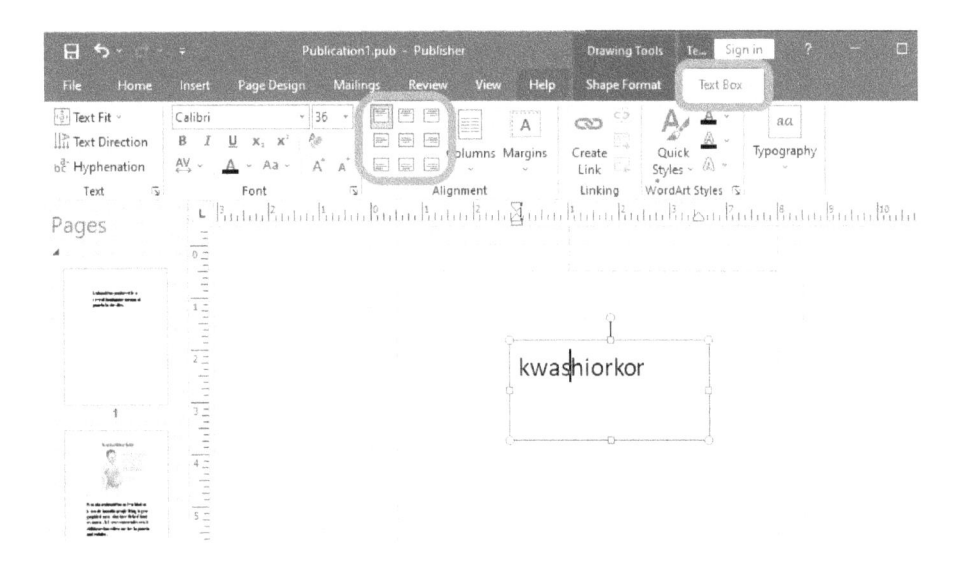

How To Join Text Boxes

As you are working with the text boxes, You might find out that a text box is not big enough to require all of the tests you want to include. You can also connect the boxes when you run out of room for text. Text will overflow or proceed from one text box to the next, once two or more text boxes are joined. Choose your 'text box tools' format ribbon, and tick 'create a link'.

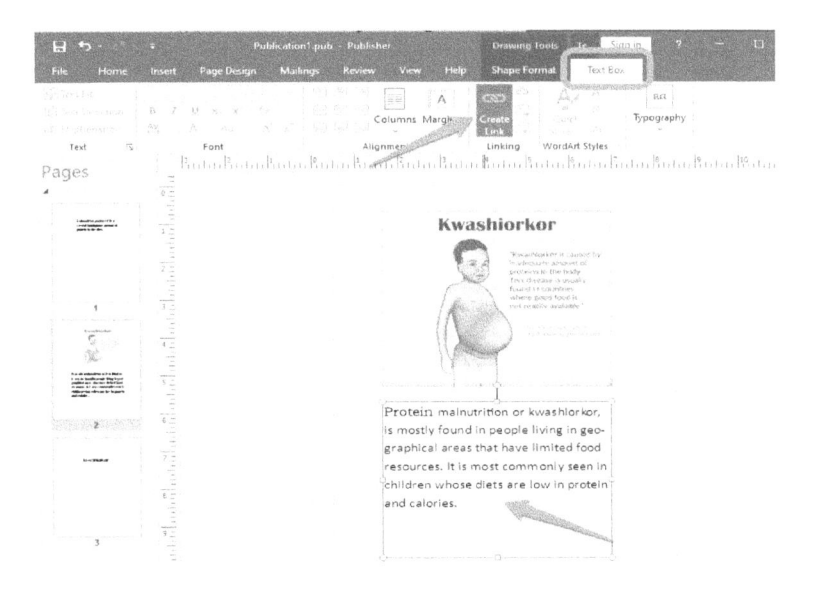

The pointer of your mouse will change into a 'link icon'. Tick the position on your page where you like to link to.

A new test box will appear, As you type your text, the text will overflow onto the order text box.

Chapter Three
Getting Started with Tables

We have added a few more texts about the percentage of anemia in the world to our document. Right now we will add a table to illustrate our text. Go to your insert ribbon and select the table to insert a table.

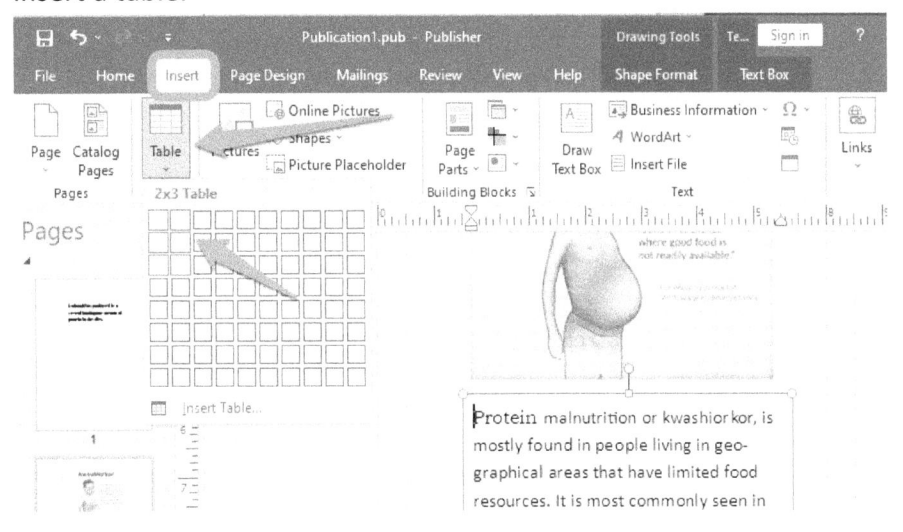

In the grid that comes over highlight the number of rows and columns you need. For this table, 1 row and 2 columns. This will add a table with 1 row and 2 columns to your document.

Drag the table into position and input your data. To navigate within cells on the table press the tab key. When you reach the end of the row, pressing the tab will add a new row.

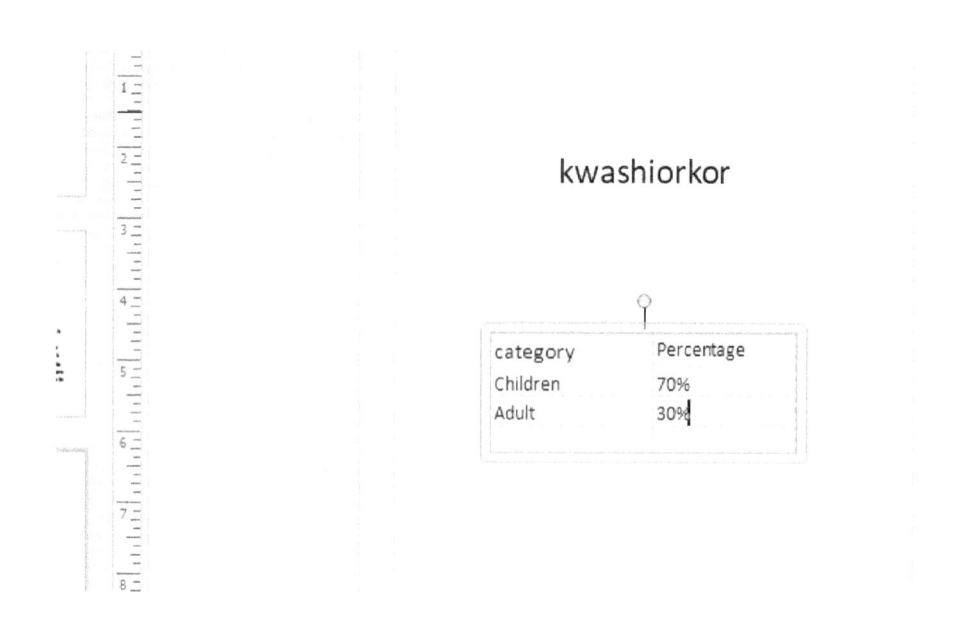

Resizing Table

Click and drag one of the corners of the grey borders To resize a table.

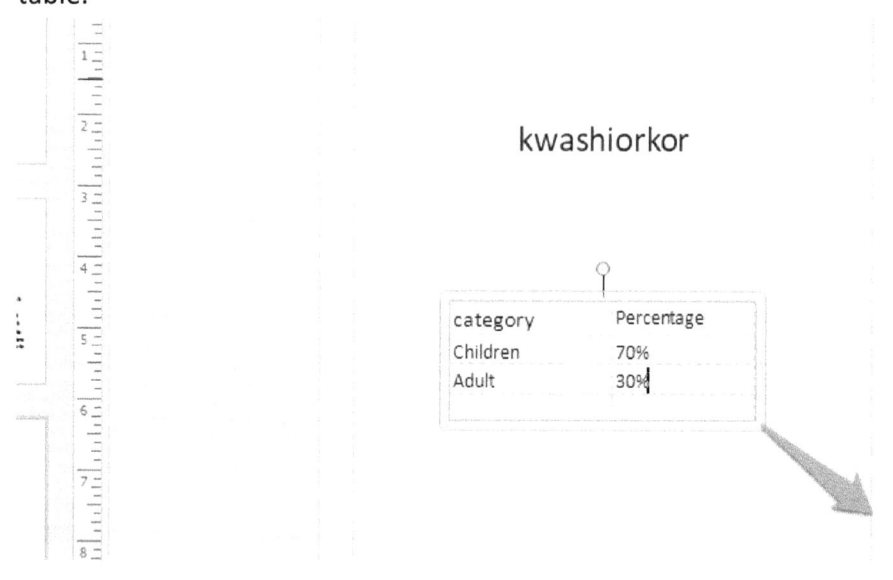

50

Moving Table

To move your table, just click anywhere on the table, then click and drag the border.

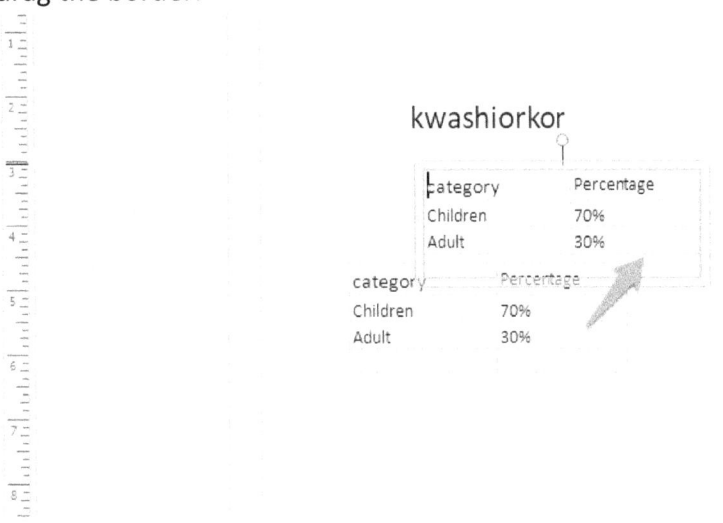

Formatting Your Tables

Immediately you click on the table in your document, two new ribbons will come over below 'table tools': design and layout. The design ribbon will permit you to select pre-set designs for your tables, such as borders, color, column, and row shading. At the center of your design ribbon, you will discover a list of designs. Click on the small arrow at the bottom right of the 'tables styles' panel to open it up.

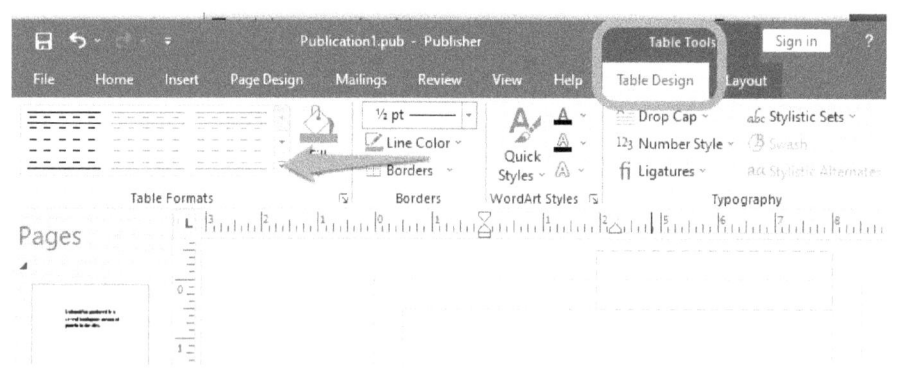

For this table, I will choose one with shaded rows and blue headings.

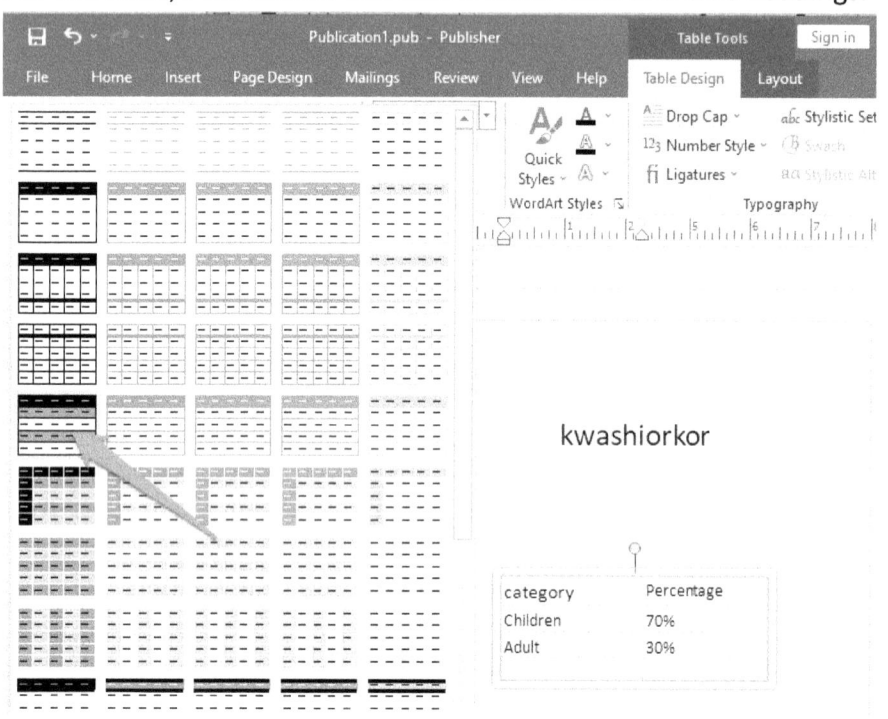

Adding a Column

You can add a column to the right-hand side of your table. To do this, click inside the end column

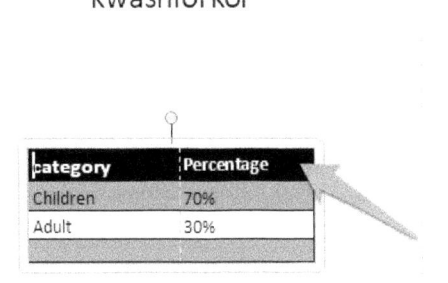

Select the layout ribbon under 'table tools', and select 'insert right'.

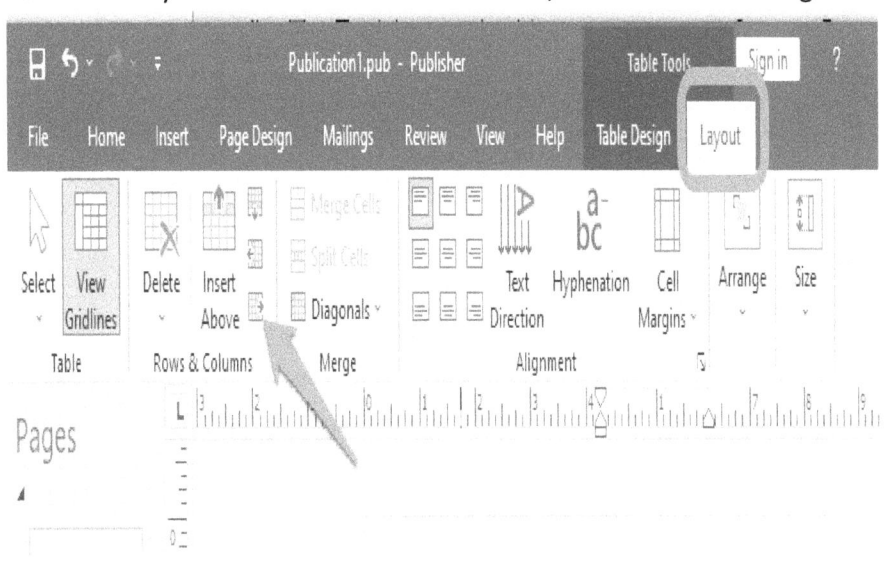

Inserting a Row

to insert a row, click on the row where you want to insert it. I want to add a row between pregnant women and women 15-49. So click on women 15-49, as shown
below.

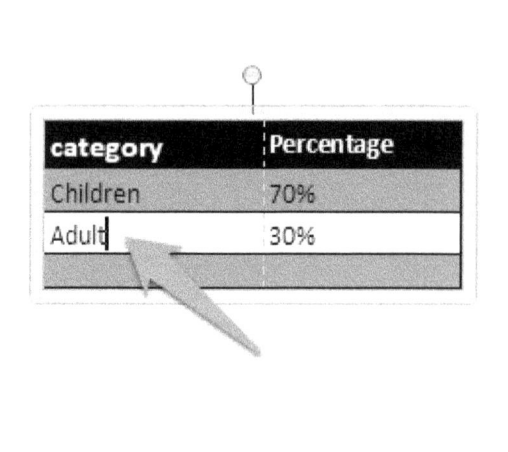

Click on the layout ribbon from the table tools section.

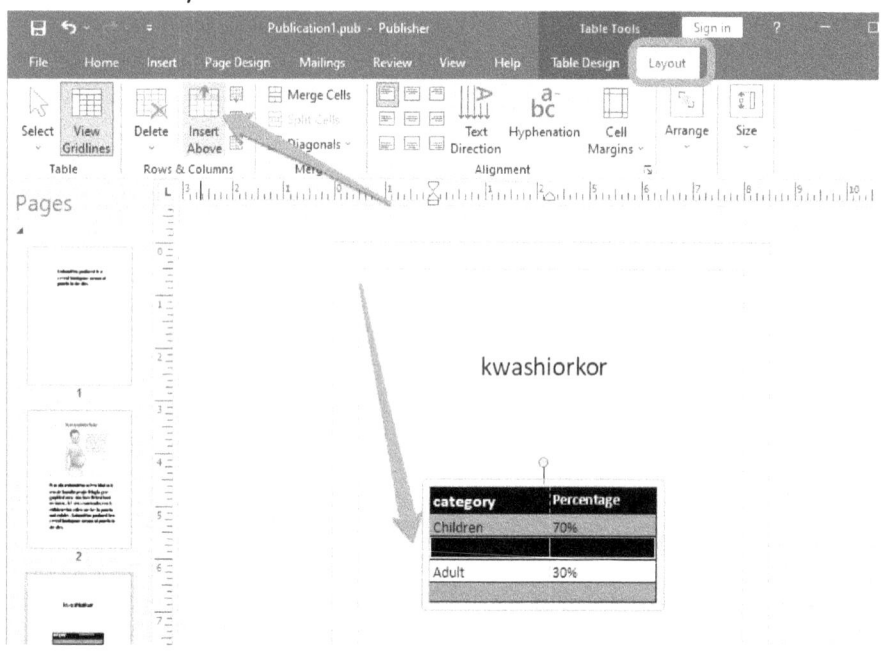

Click 'insert above'. This will input a row above the one chosen earlier.

54

Resizing Rows & Columns

To resize the row and column you can do that by clicking and dragging the row and column splitting line to the size you want.

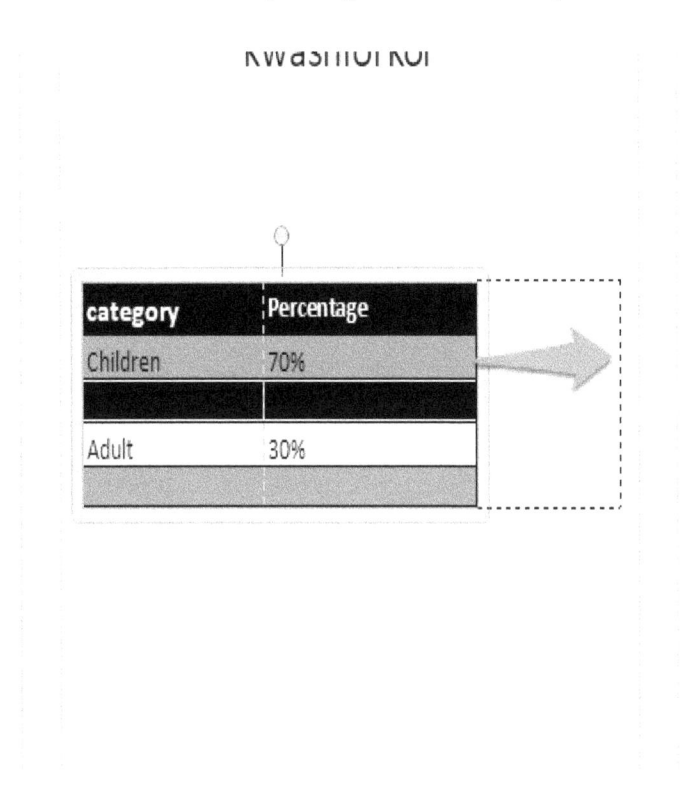

Merge cells

You can merge cells by following the steps below:
1. Select and highlight the cells you want to merge.
2. Then select 'merge cells' from the ribbon in the table tools section.

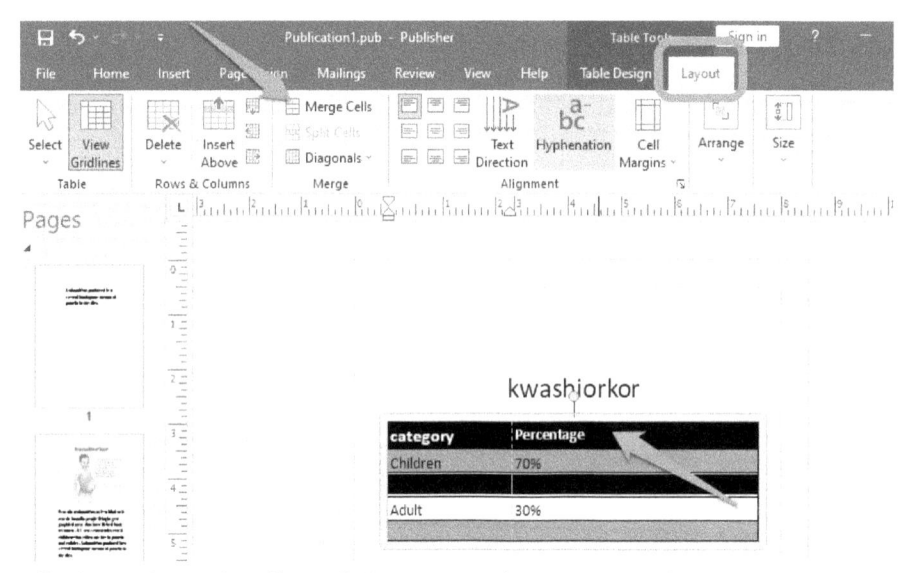

All the selected cells will be merged into a single one as shown below.

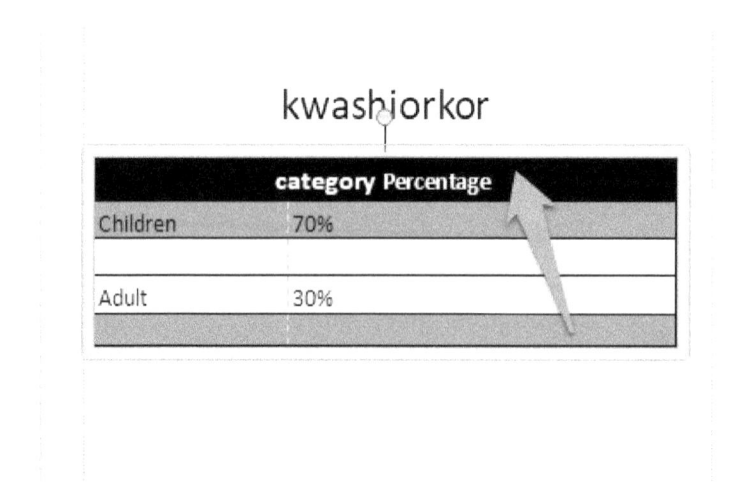

Align Cell Text

For you to be able to change the text alignment in the cells of the table, the first thing is to select the cells you want to align. Click and drag.

kwashiorkor

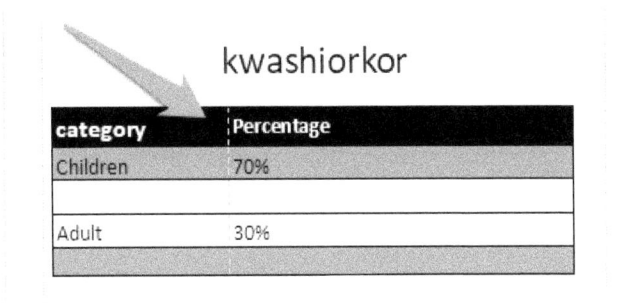

category	Percentage
Children	70%
Adult	30%

Then select the layout ribbon in the table tools section, as shown under.

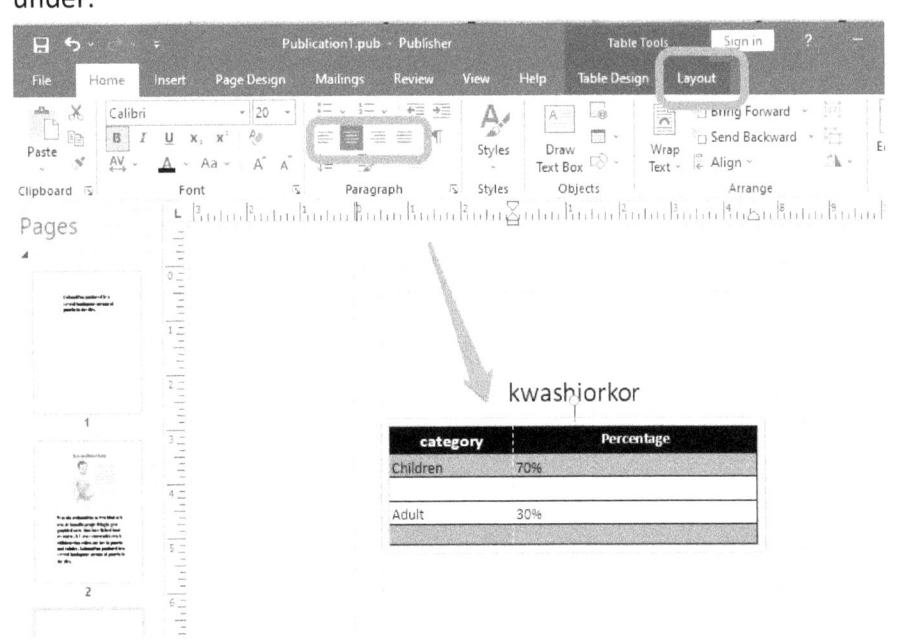

kwashiorkor

category	Percentage
Children	70%
Adult	30%

From the alignment section, make use of the nine boxes to select the text alignment you want to assign to the cells.

Below is a quick guide to what the nine diverse alignments look like. In the diagram beneath, note where every single box on the left puts the text in the cells in the example on the right.

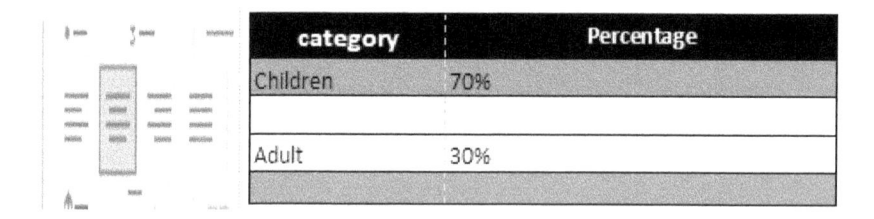

For example, select the center box to align the cells to the center of the cell.

Adding Cell Border

pick the cells you want to add a border to.

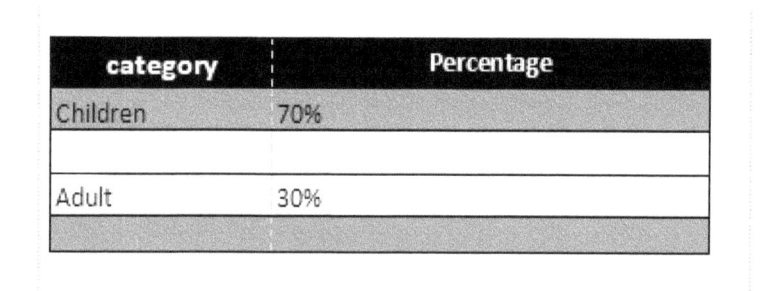

Click the 'table tools' design tab. Choose a line thickness

choose a line color

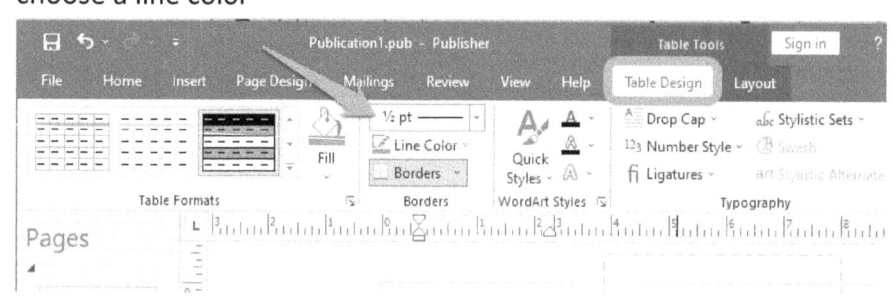

58

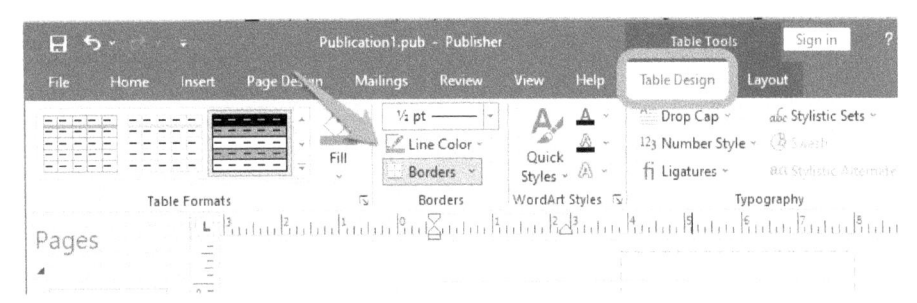

Click on the 'borders'. From the drop-down list, choose where on your selection you want the borders to come into sight.

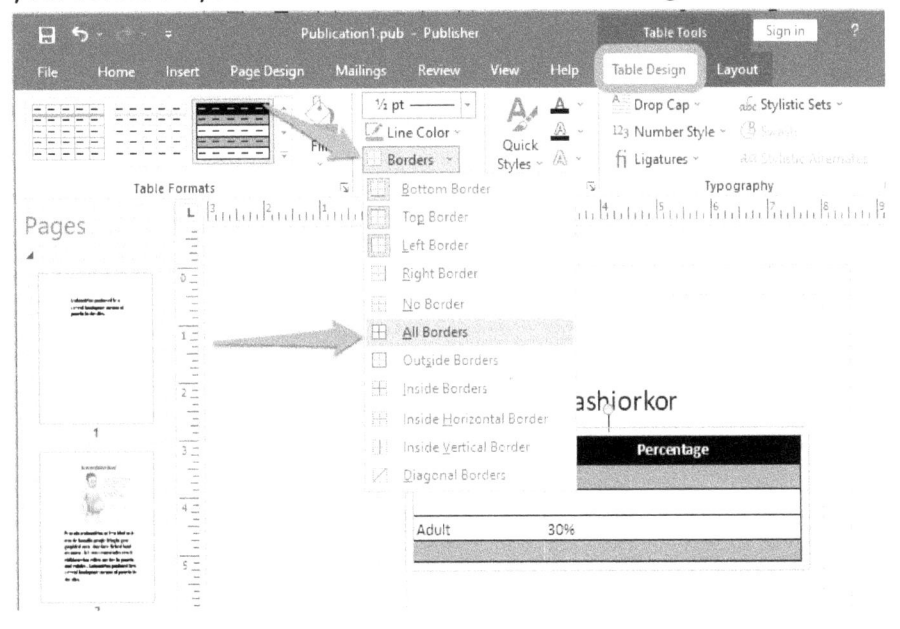

Changing Cell Color

choose the cell or cells you want to change color

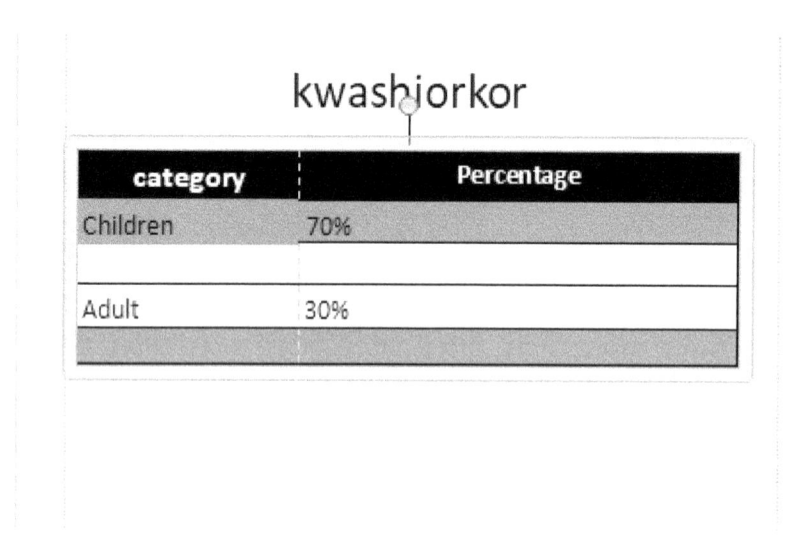

choose the 'table tools' design tab.

Click on the fill. Then choose a color from the pallet.

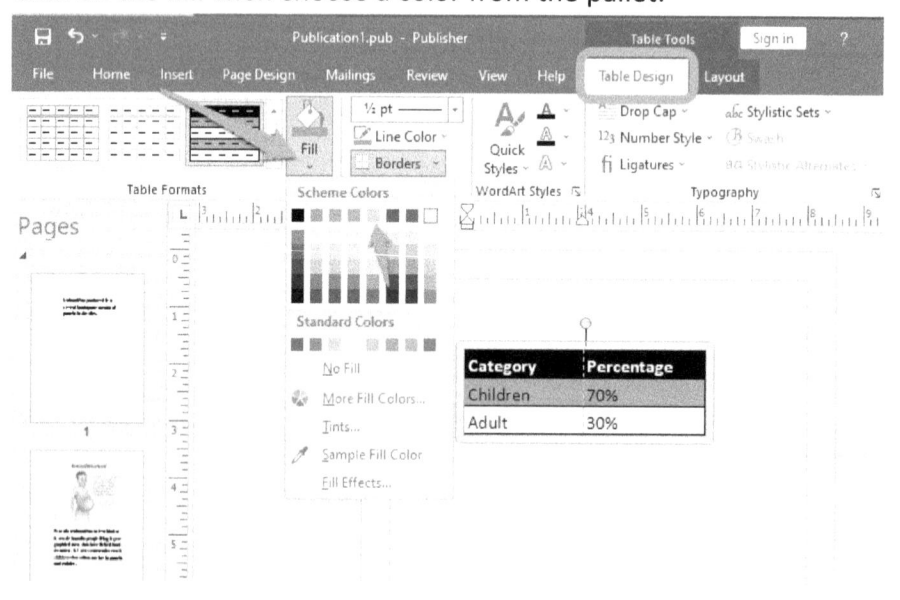

Text Direction

You can organize the text vertically, this works for the headings most of the time

To do this, select the heading rows in your table.

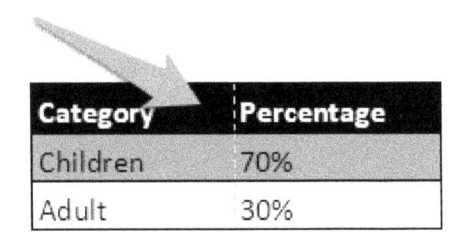

Then click 'text direction' from the layout ribbon.

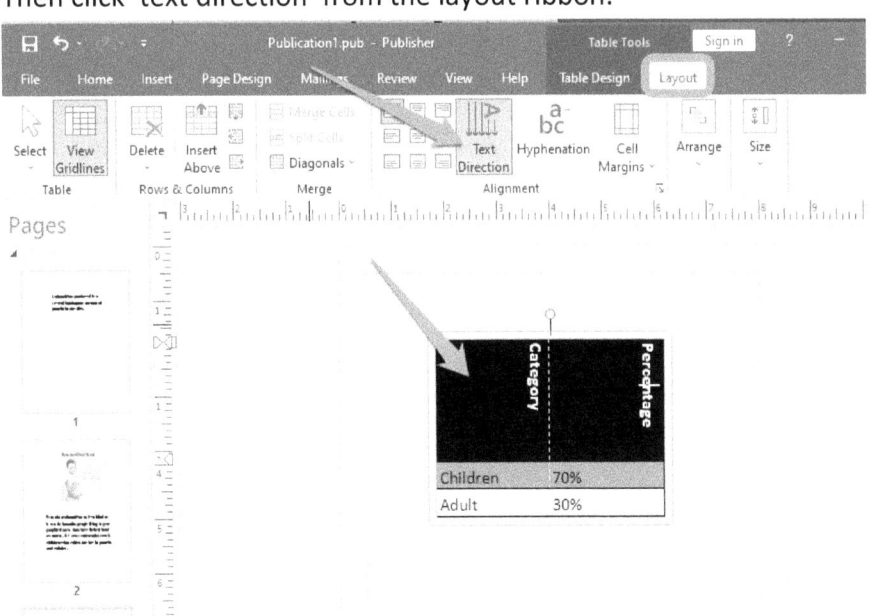

Chapter Four
Operating Graphics

Under this segment, we will be examining how to add shapes, images, and other tools to add some color to our publication.

Including images

For you to add pictures to your document is easy. You can find two ways you can include images to your document, your pictures, and photos saved on your OneDrive or computer.

Go to your 'insert ribbon' and tap on 'pictures'.

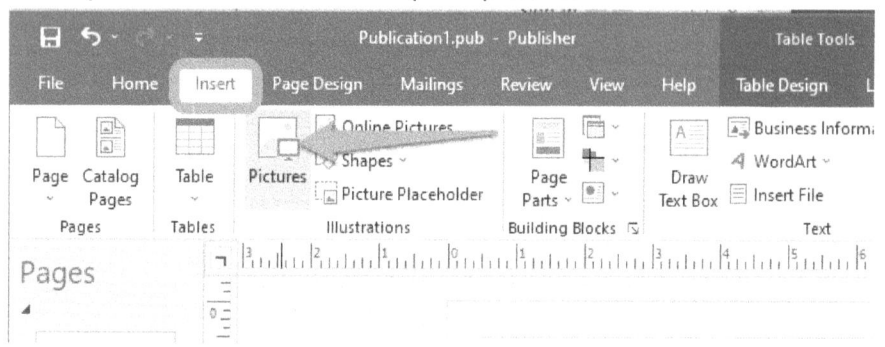

Choose the picture or photo you desire to use from the dialog box that shows up. Tap Insert. This will bring your photo into your document. See the image below:

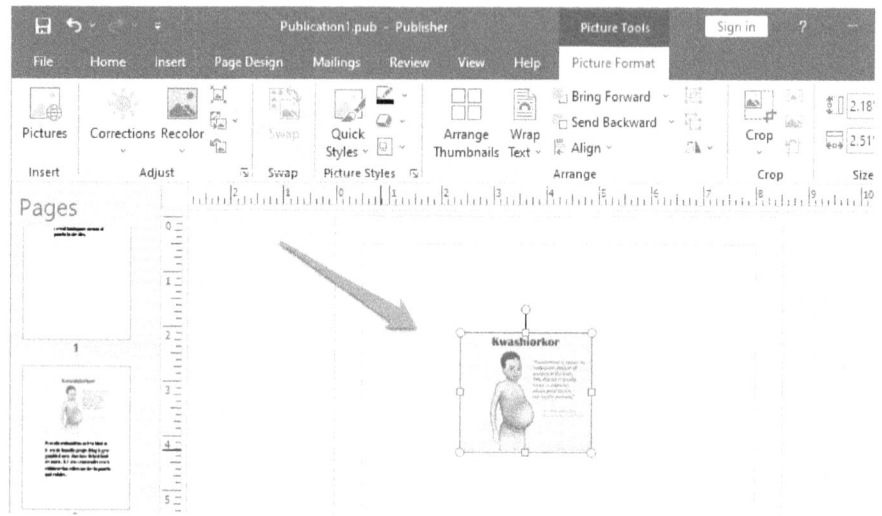

You may need to rescale the photo, once included in the publisher, as occasionally they can come in a little big. To accomplish this tick on the image or picture, and you will discover little handles emerge on each angle of the image. These are known as resize handles. They can be applied by taping and dragging a corner in the direction of the center of the image to make it tinier as shown beneath. Press the shift key as you rescale the image to obstruct it from being distorted.

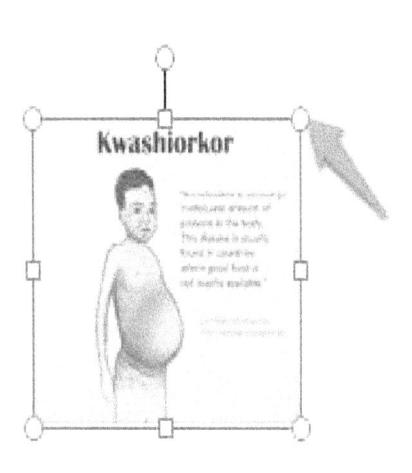

Tick and drag the photo into position on your document.

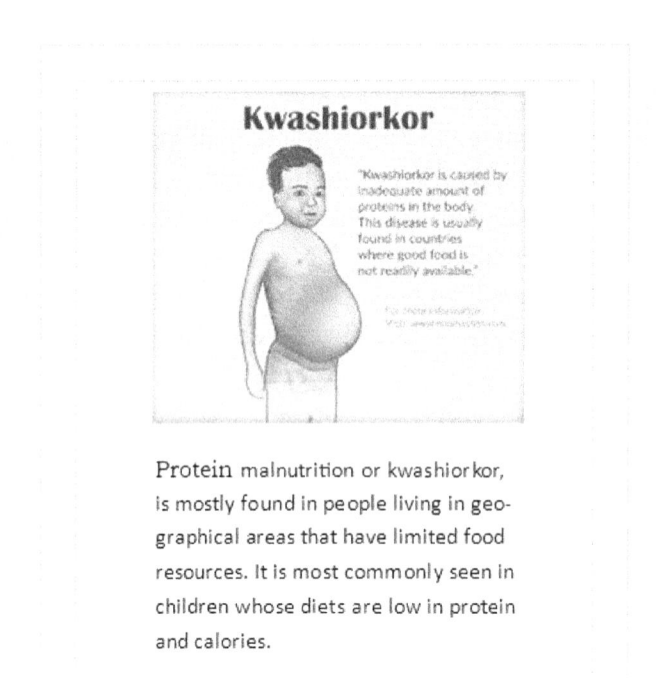

Protein malnutrition or kwashiorkor, is mostly found in people living in geographical areas that have limited food resources. It is most commonly seen in children whose diets are low in protein and calories.

Image Out of Google

You can look for images on Google. After downloading an image, be sure to store it in your pictures folder. Open your web browser and start a Google search, afterward pick 'images'.

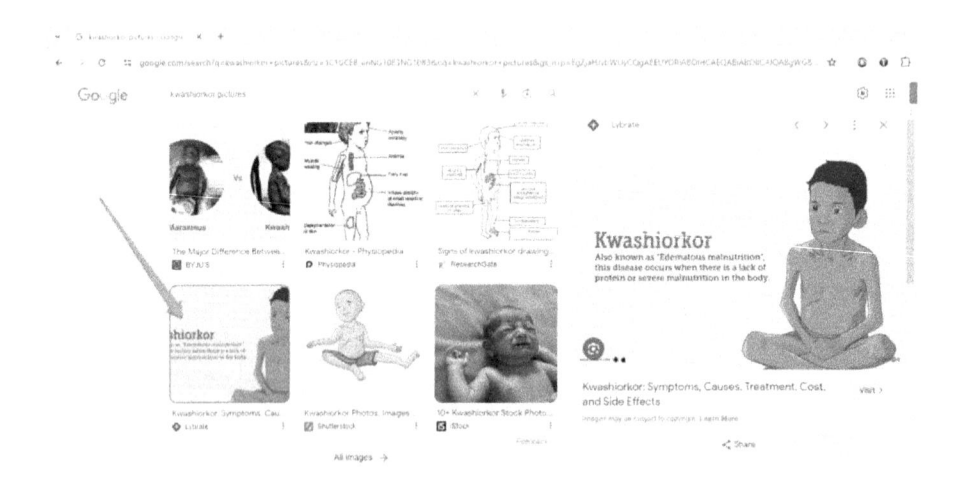

Tick the image thumbnail in the search results to see the full-size image. Right-click the image, then pick 'save image as' from the popup list.

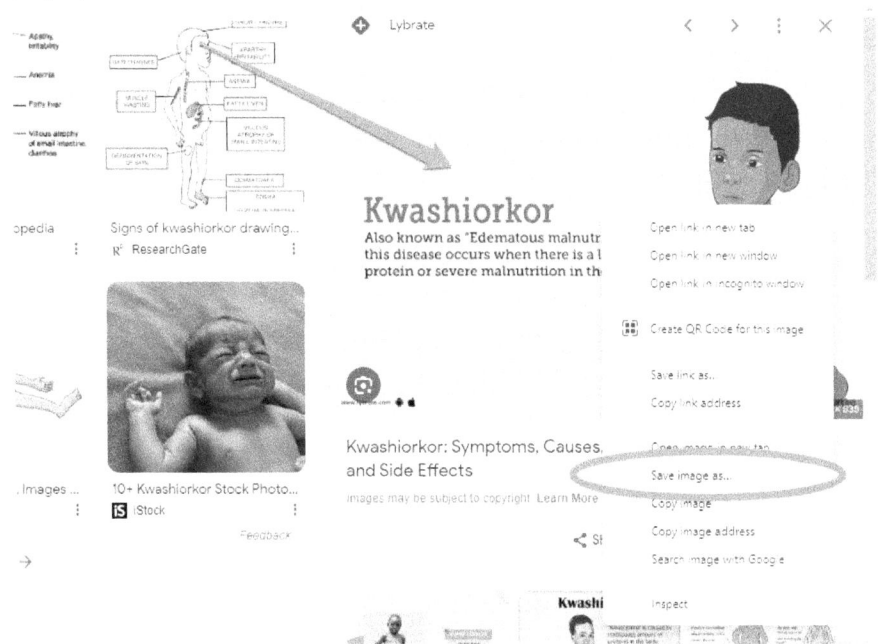

From the dialog box that comes in view, store the image in your 'picture folder' either on your PC or on your OneDrive folder.

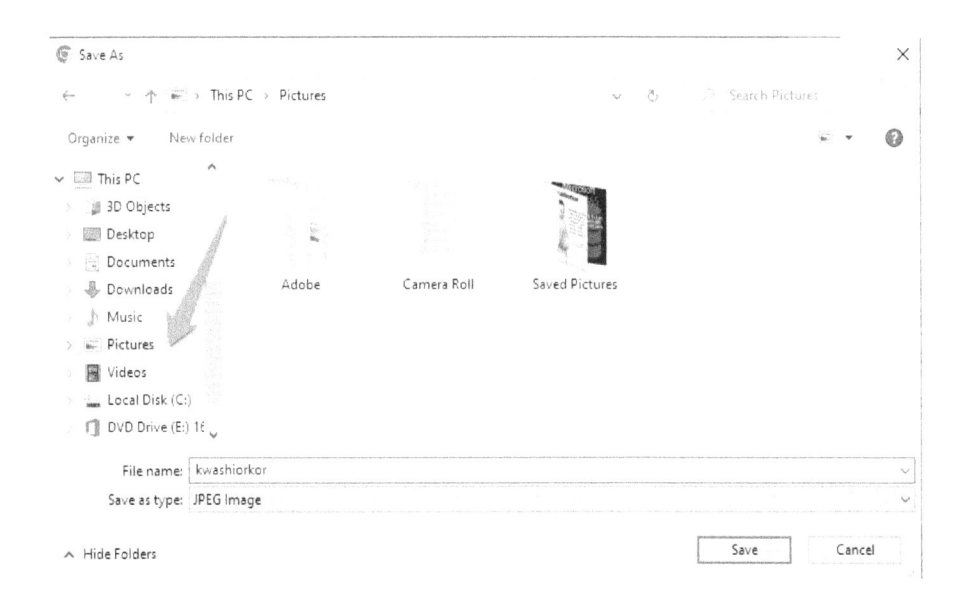

As soon as your image is stored in your pictures folder, you can bring them into your Publisher document making use of the same procedures at the start of the chapter.

Inserting clipart

To continue with our document, I will be introducing a new section known as **Worldwide Percentage of Anemia** and I require some clipart to describe this.

To insert a clipart picture, go to your insert ribbon and tick 'online pictures'.

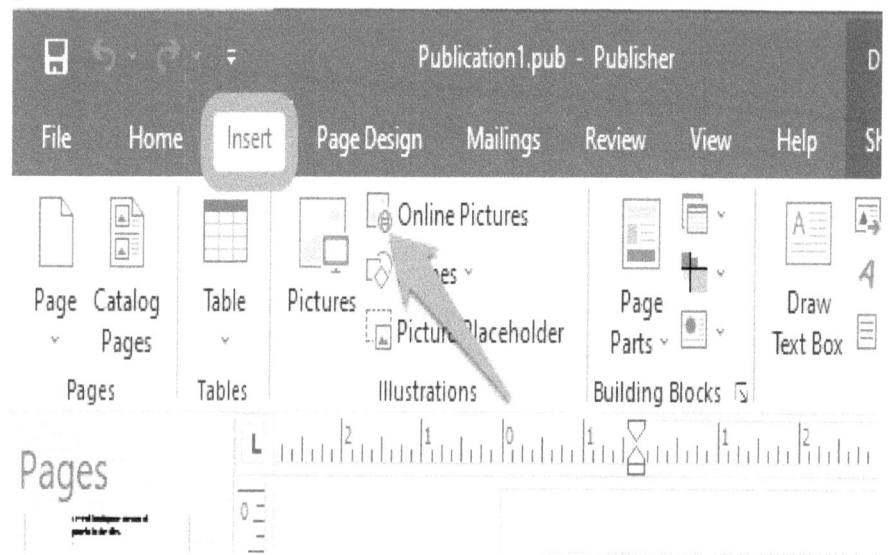

Then put in what you are seeking in the dialog box, as shown beneath. Under this example, put in the search term 'kwashiorkor'

Consider this, you will require an internet connection for you to be able to get what you are seeking.

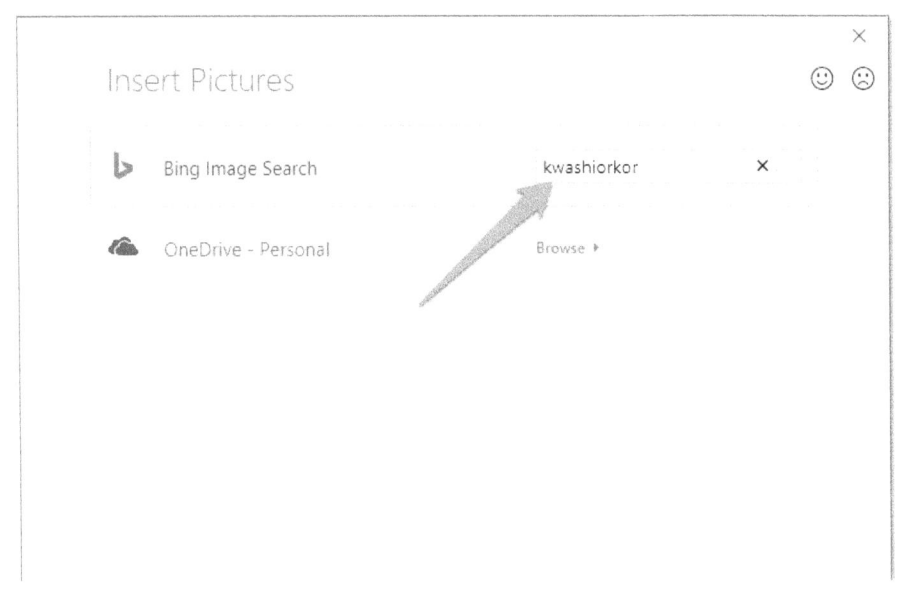

In the search outcomes, pick the image you require then tap Insert.

You might wish to modify and set the image. Press the shift key as you modify the image to halt it from being deformed.

Including Effects on Images

To include effects to your images, such as borders and shadows, tick on your image, and choose the 'Pictures tools' format tab. In this illustration, tick on the kwashiorkor image.

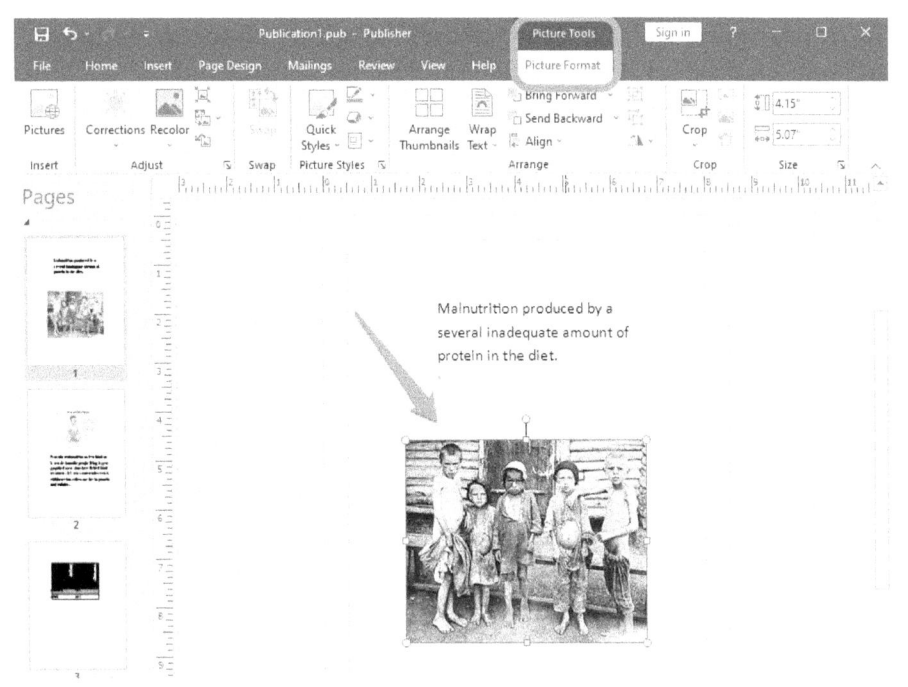

I would like to produce a nice reflection style for the image. To do this, I will tick on 'picture effects', then progress to 'reflection'. Choose a variation as shown below.

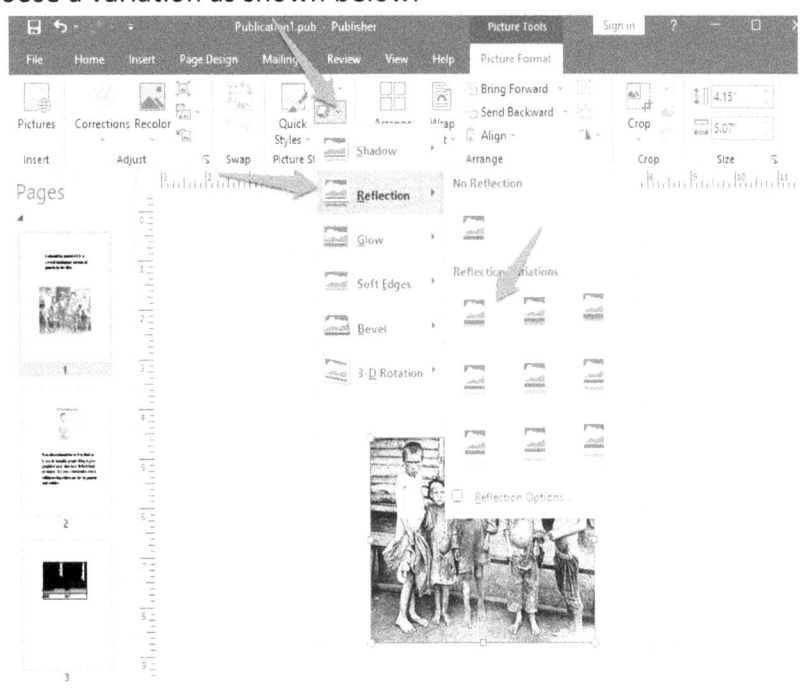

You can attempt various effects, such as **glow, shadow, or bevel. Find out** what effect they have.

Insert a Caption

You need to tick the image you want to insert the caption to, from the 'picture tools' format ribbon pick 'caption'. Then from the drop-down list, choose a caption style.

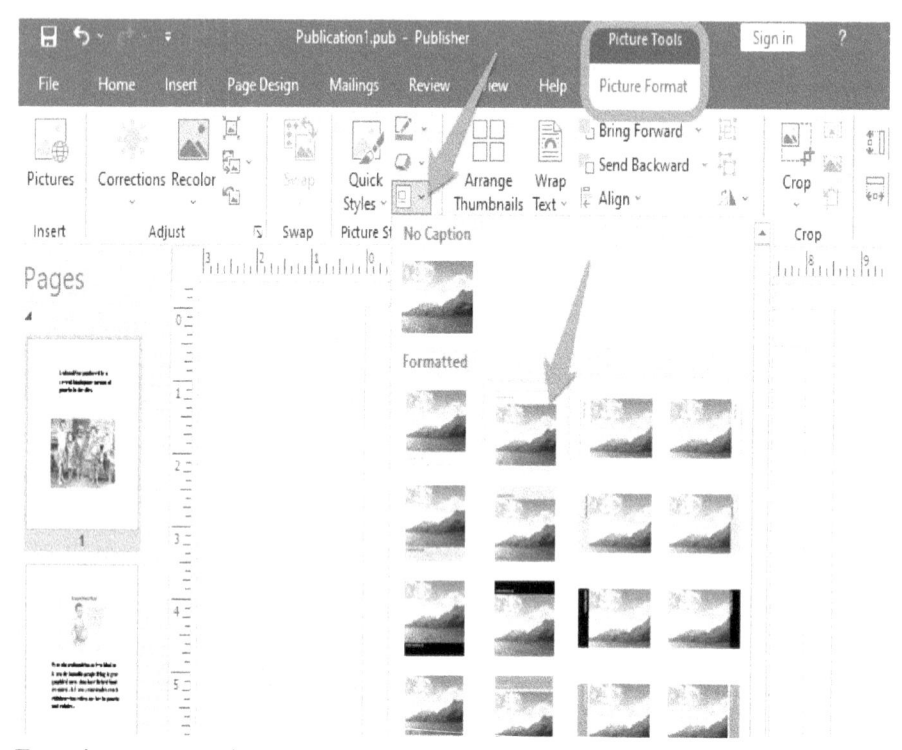

Type in your caption.

Cropping Images

For example, if you bring an image into your document, and you realize it has a portion you don't want or you want to give attention to one particular area of the image, you can crop the image.

Foremost, bring an image from your pictures library into your document.

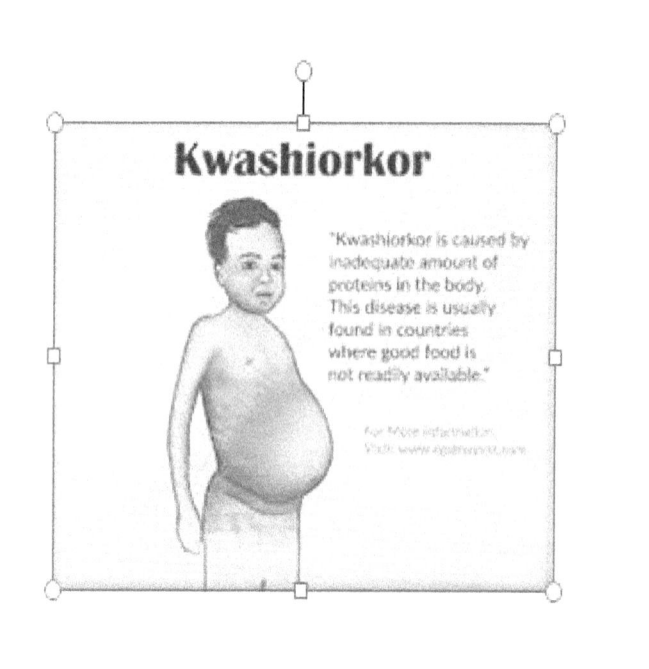

To crop, tick on the image, then tap the 'picture tools' format tab. From the format ribbon, tick the crop icon.

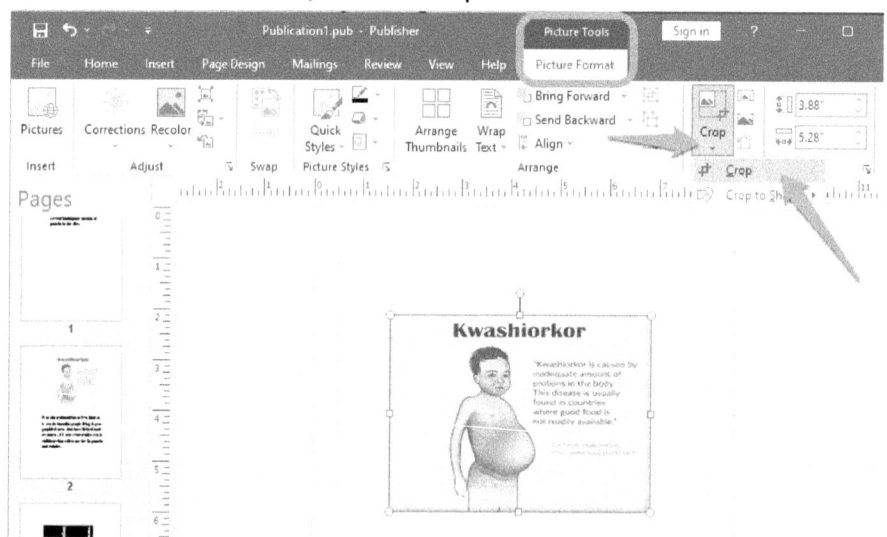

If you observe around your image, you will see crop handles around the edges, as displayed beneath.

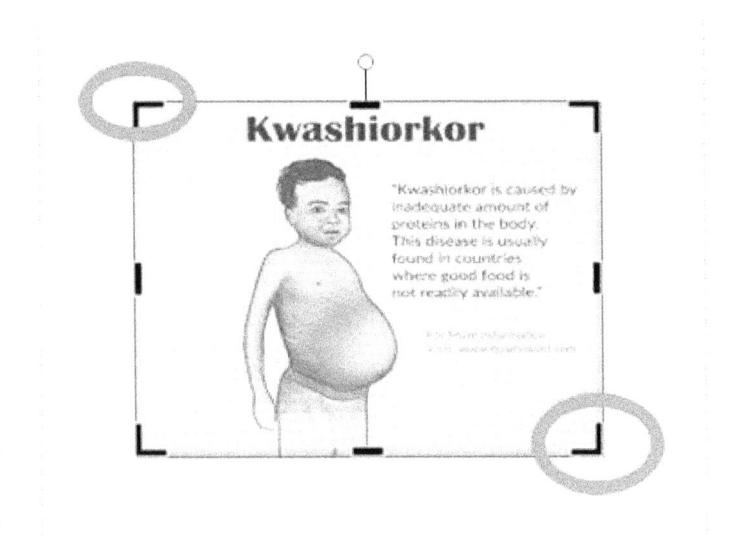

Tick and move these handles around the area of the image you want. For, I would like to save Kwashiorkor in the image.

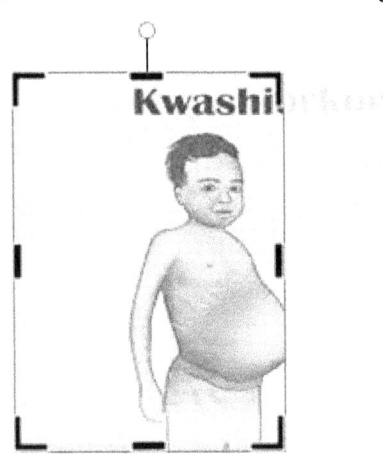

Tick anywhere on your document to finalize, the light grey bits will be cut off to make the bit of the image inside the crop square.

Cropping to form

For you to crop an image to suit within a form. First, put an image from your pictures library into your document.

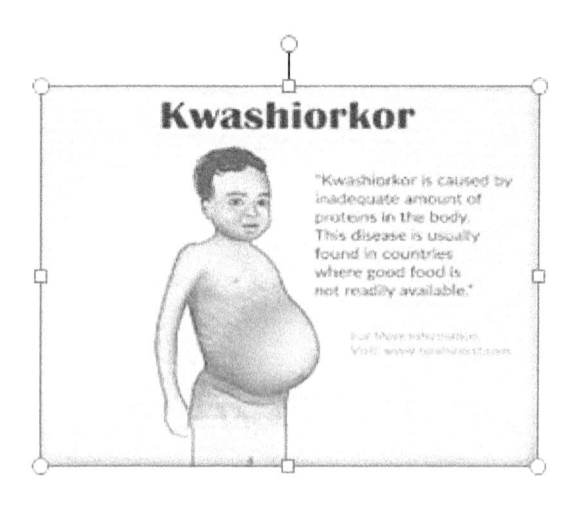

To produce this abide by the steps beneath:
1. Tick on the image.
2. Then tick on the 'picture tools' format tab.
3. Tick on the down arrow below the crop icon.
4. Choose 'crop to shape' From the drop-down menu

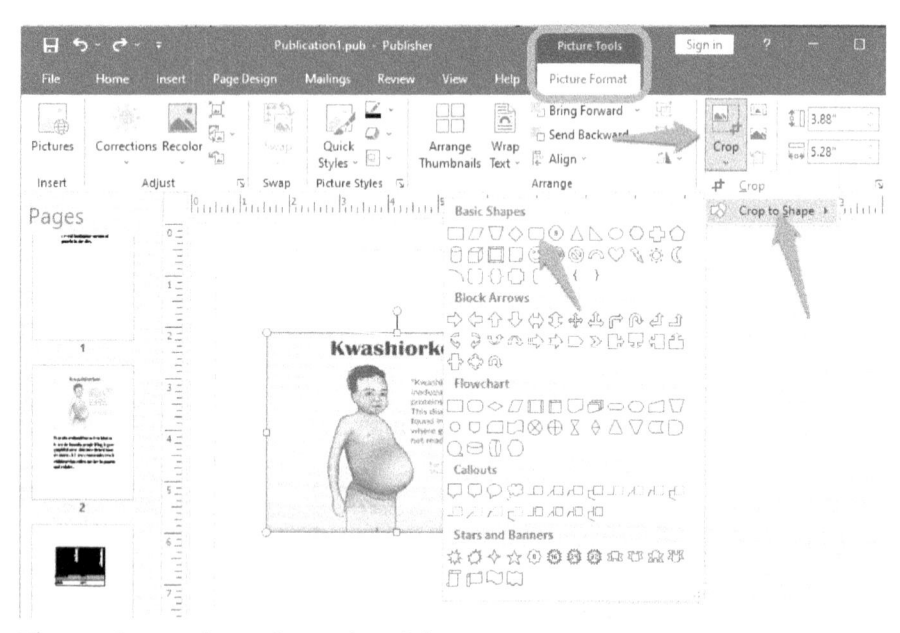

Then select a shape from the slideout.

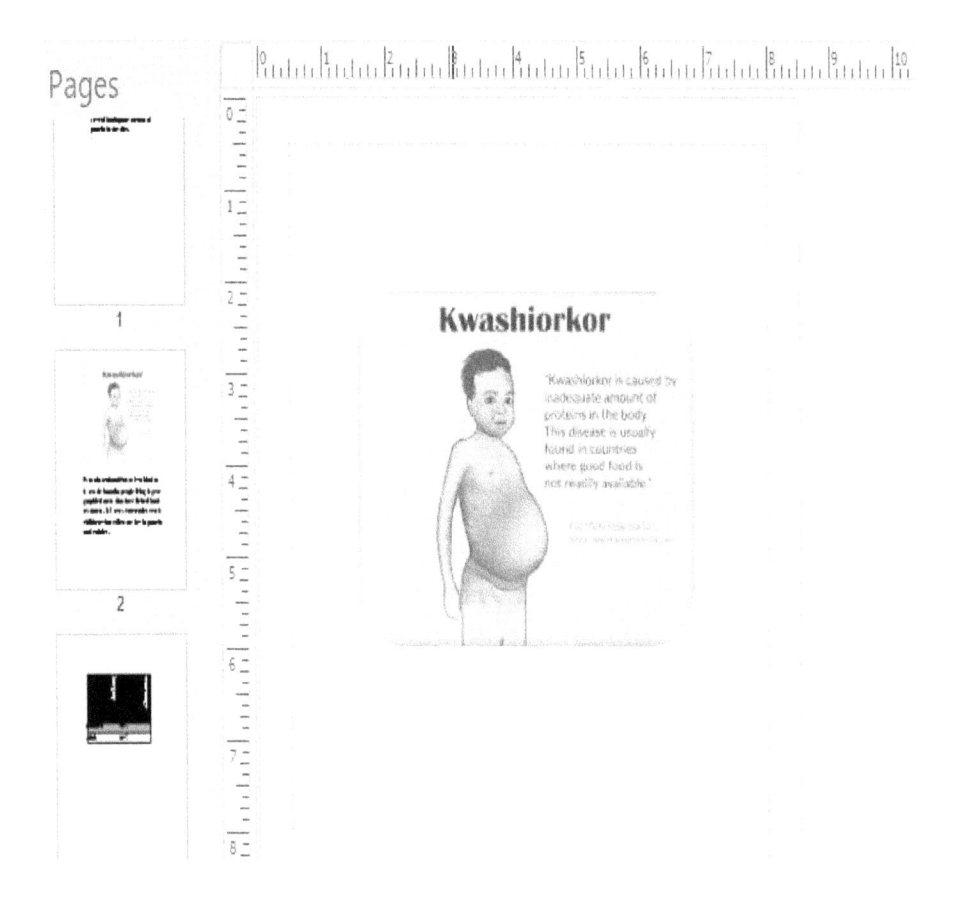

Readjusting Your Images

You can change the contrast and brightness of your images or re-color them so that the image will be inserted into your color blueprint. To adjust or control an image pay attention to the steps beneath.

1. Right-click on the image.
2. Choose 'format picture'. From the popup list.
3. Select the 'picture' tab from the dialog box.

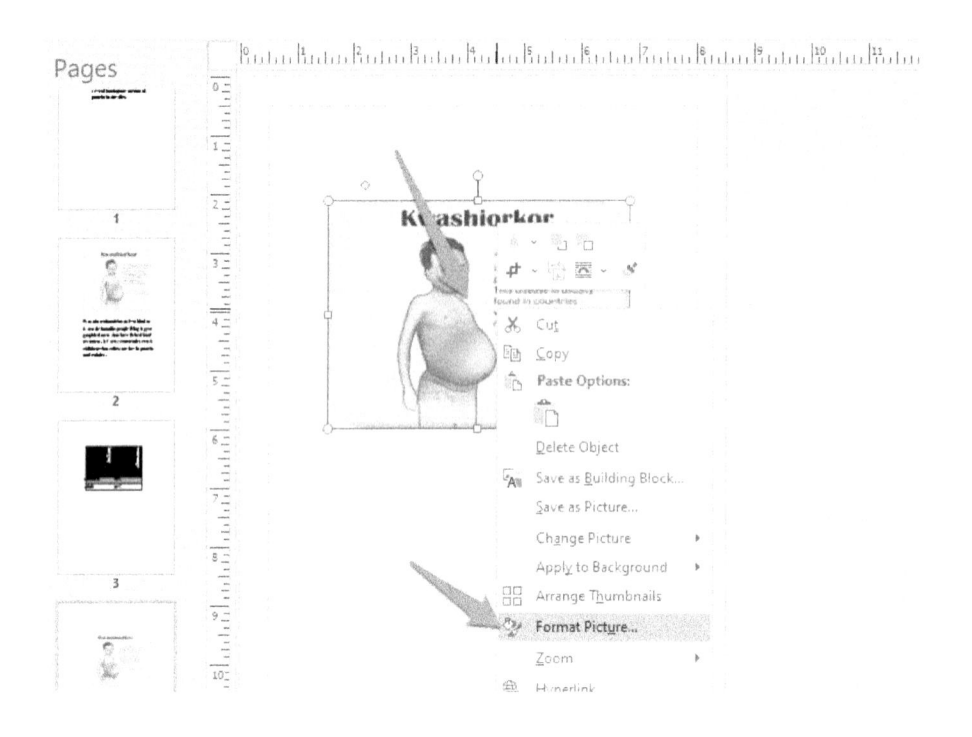

The transparency slider can now be used to modify the transparency of the image. Use the contrast and brightness sliders to modify the contrast and brightness. To alter the color of the image, use the re-color drop-down.

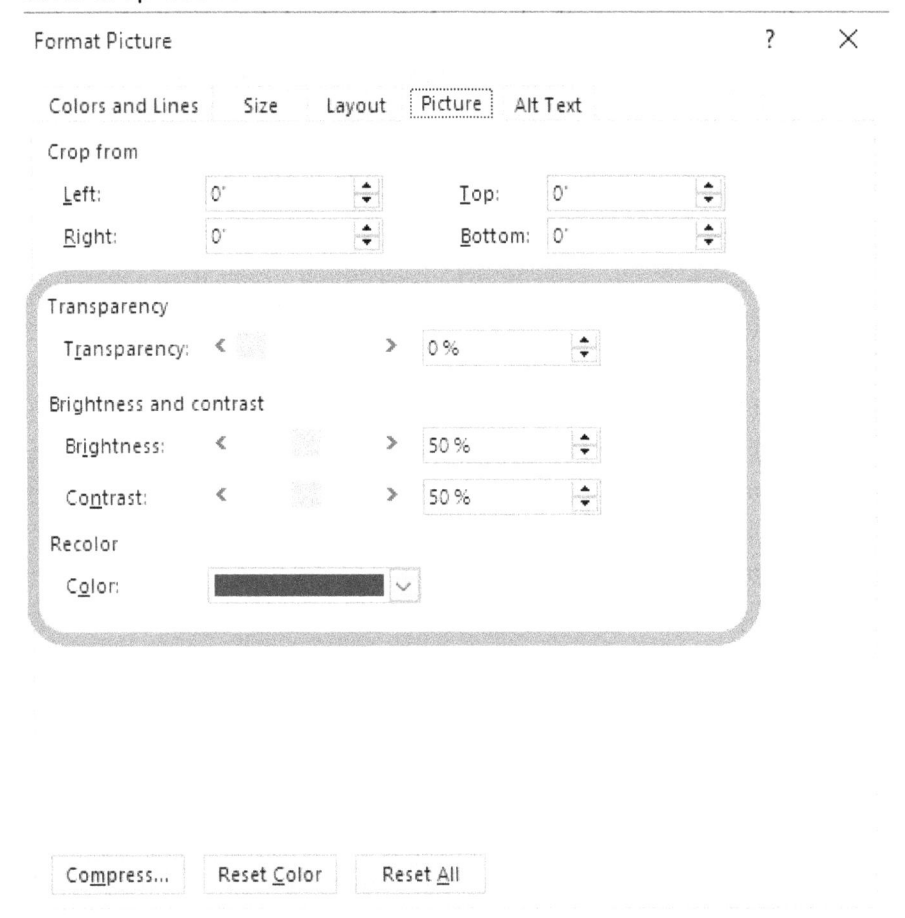

Tap 'ok' when you are through.

Wrapping Text around images

When you bring in an image, the image will be wrapped naturally with text, i.e. the text will place itself around the image instead of over it or below it.

Abide by the steps beneath, to adjust the text wrap
1. Tap on the image.
2. Tap 'wrap text' from the format tab.
3. Choose 'tight' from the drop-down menu to organize the text accurately around the border of the image.
4. Tap and pull the image into place if you want to. You will notice that the text will align itself around the image.

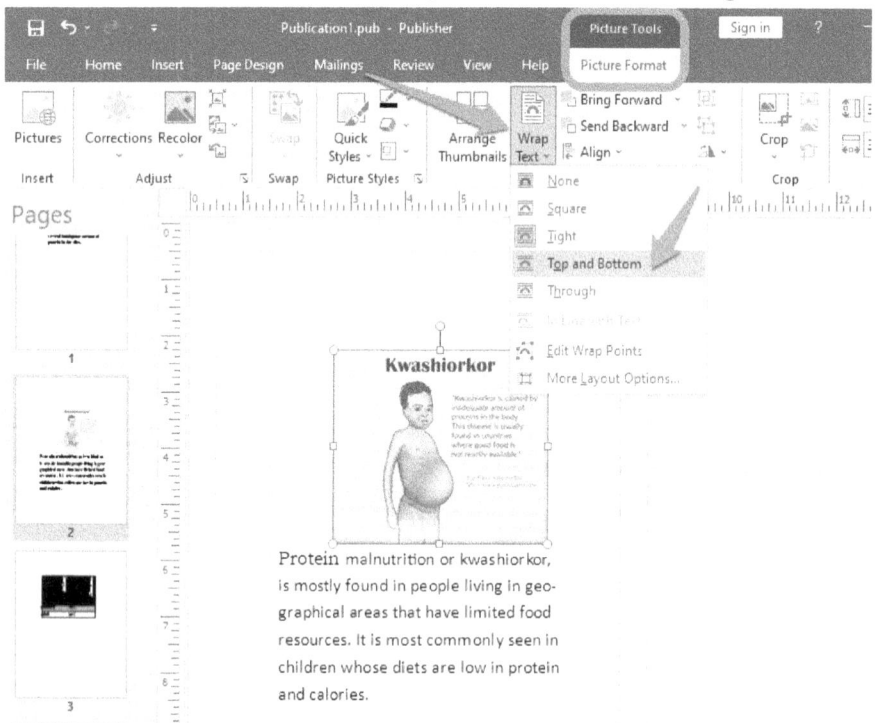

The Wrap points

Abide by the steps beneath if you want to create the points at which the text wraps the image.

1. Tap on the image
2. Tap 'wrap text' from the format ribbon.
3. Then from the drop-down list choose 'edit wrap point'.

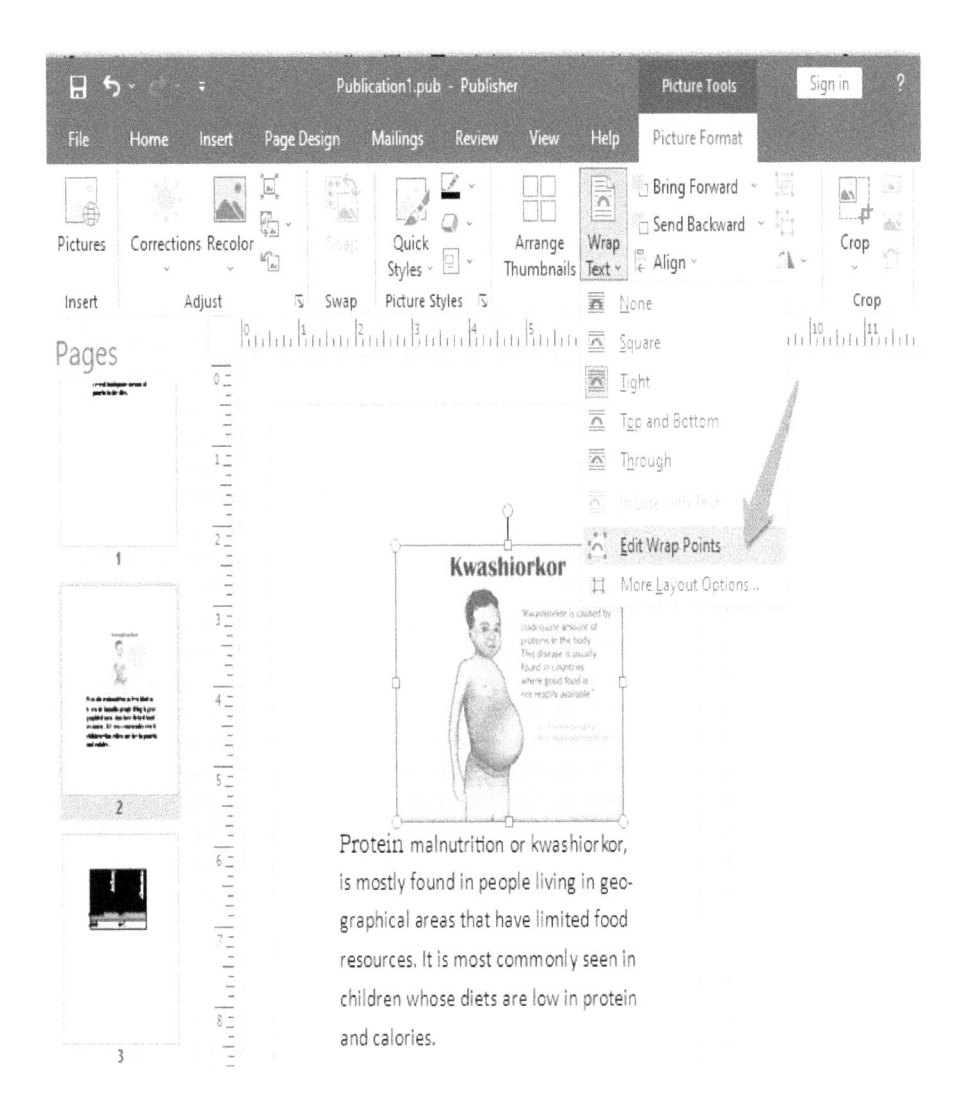

4. You will observe a dotted line appear displayed around the image. It is known as the **wrap point.** Tick and pull the dots to edit it.

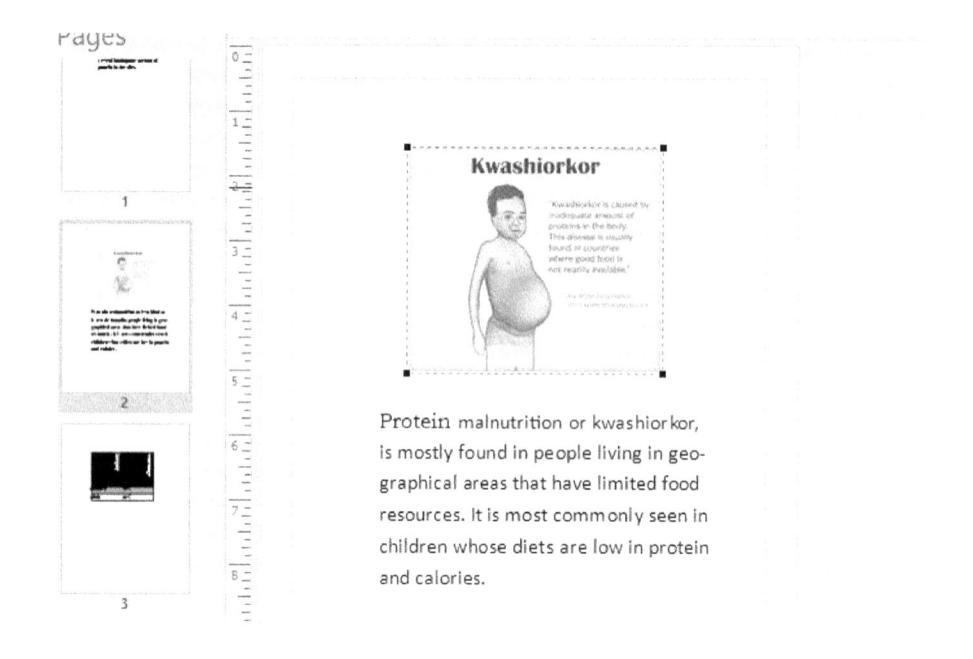

Inserting Shapes To Your Publication

You can insert various shapes into your publication. You can also insert circles, squares, lines, rectangles, and speech bubbles, you can also insert various flow chart symbols.

Tick the 'insert tab' to put in a shape.

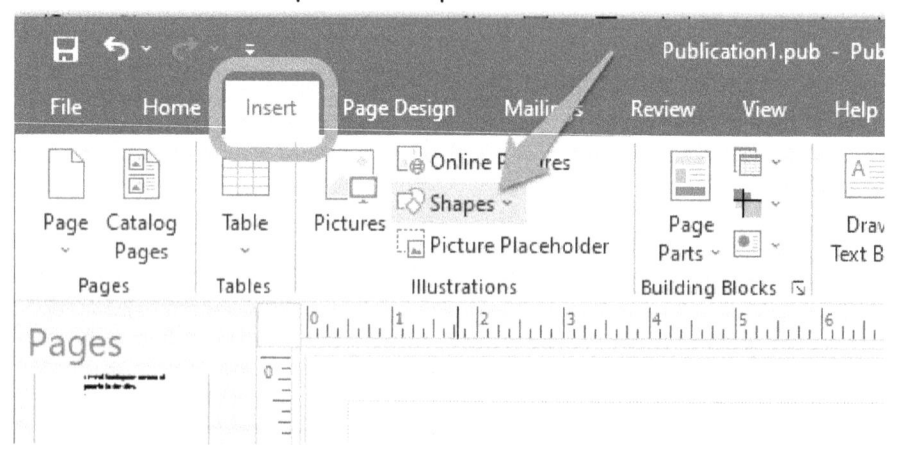

Select the shape from the drop-down menu.

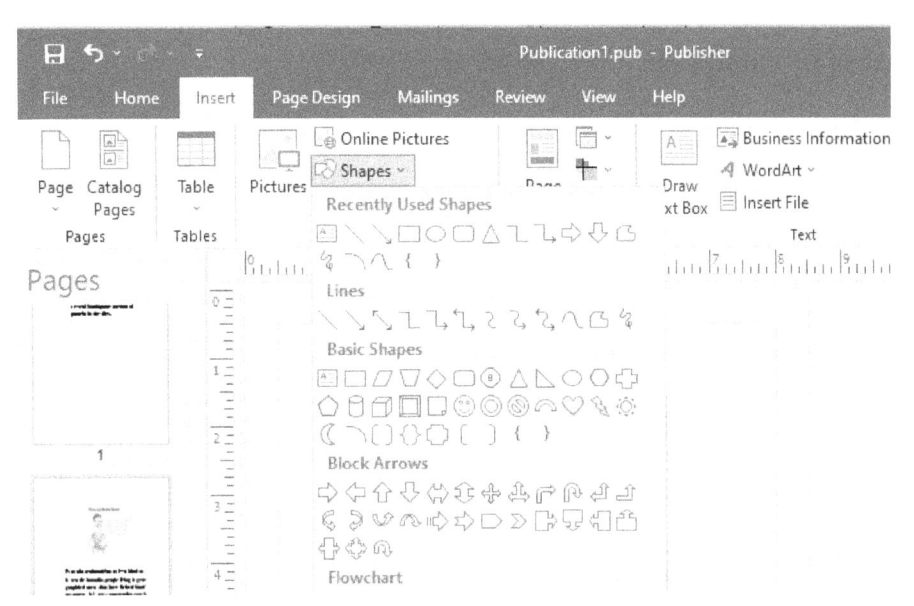

You will have to tick and pull your mouse on your document to produce your shape.

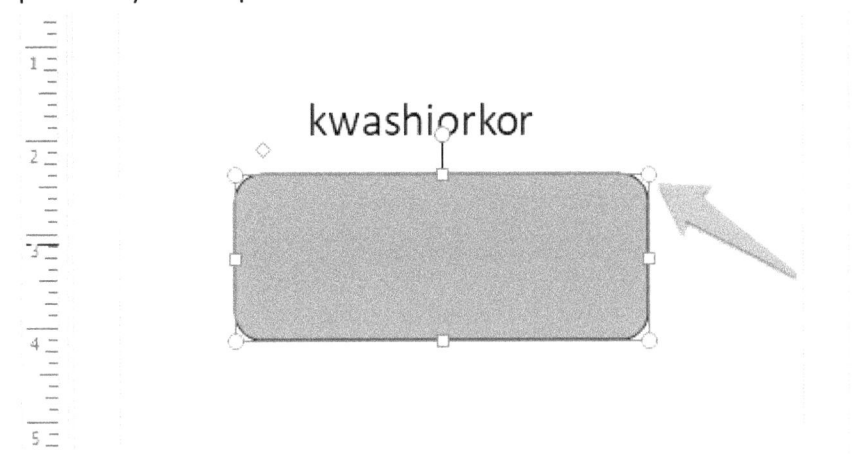

Changing Shapes

The color and the outline can be altered and shadows can be inserted shadows to your shapes.

Altering The Color

Abide by the steps below to alter this
1. Tick on the shape
2. Select the 'drawing tools' format tab.
3. Select 'fill color', then choose a color from the drop-down menu.

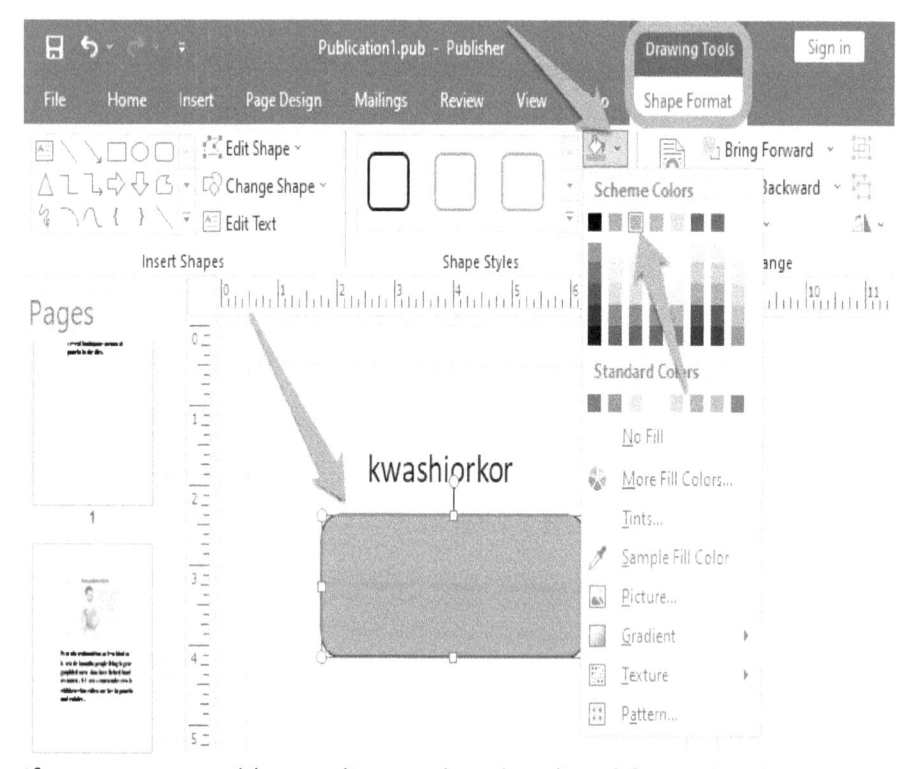

If you want to add a gradient, select 'gradient' from the drop-down menu. And if you also want to include a texture, choose 'texture'

Altering The Border

If you want to alter this, tick on your image, then choose the 'drawing tools' format tab. Select 'shape outline', then pick a color.

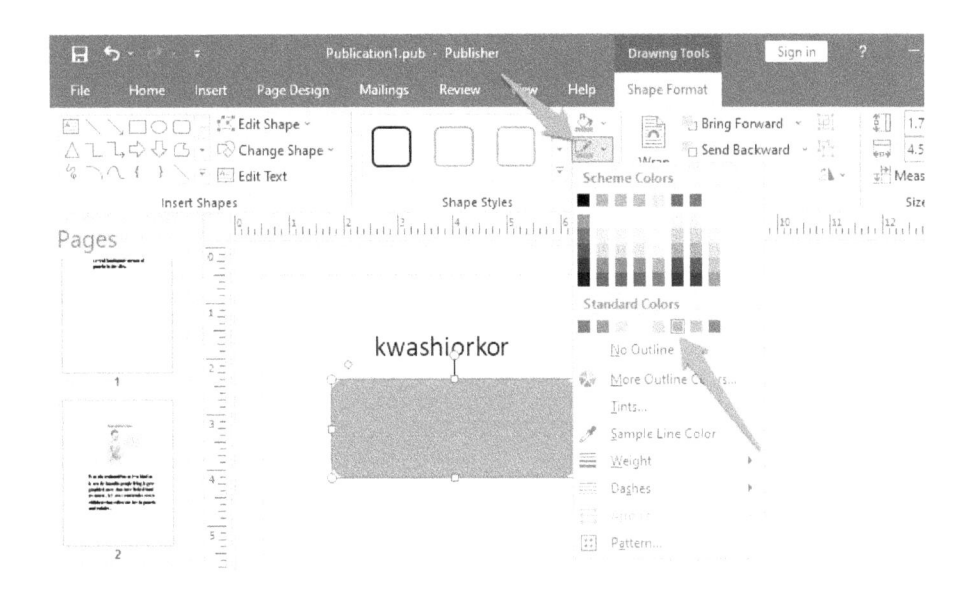

Select 'weight' if you want to alter the thickness of the border.

Including a Shadow

Tick on the image, then tap on the 'drawing tools' format tab.

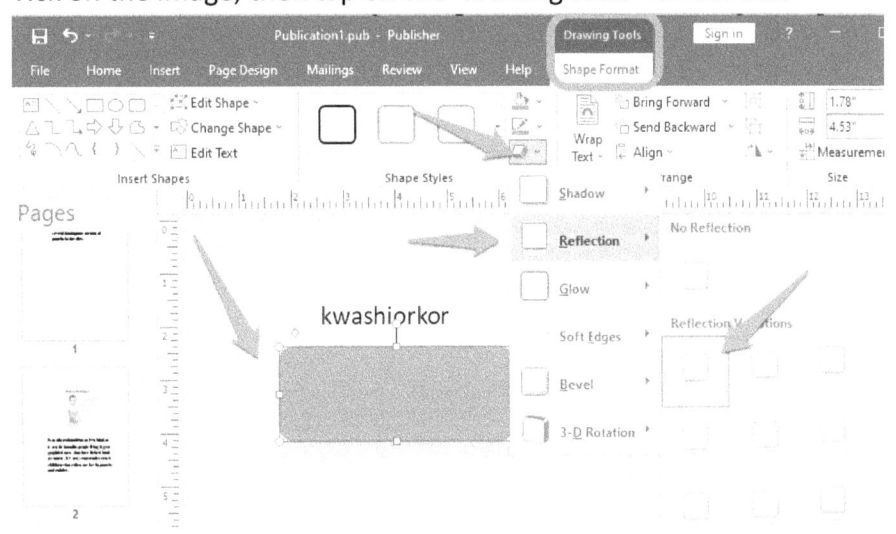

Select 'shape effects', then choose an effect from the drop-down menu. If you want to modify the effect, scroll down to 'option' at the bottom of the slideout list.

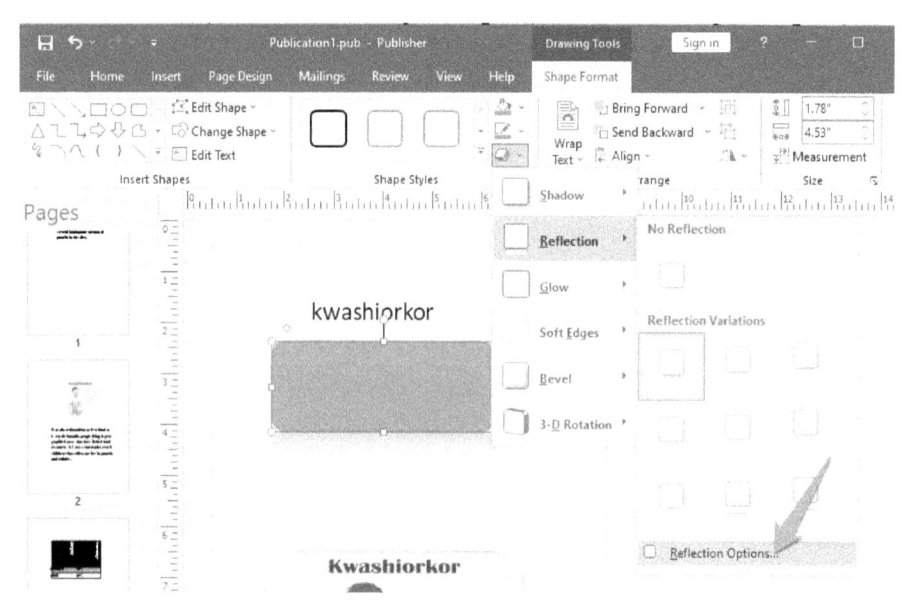

The Format Shape dialog box appears.

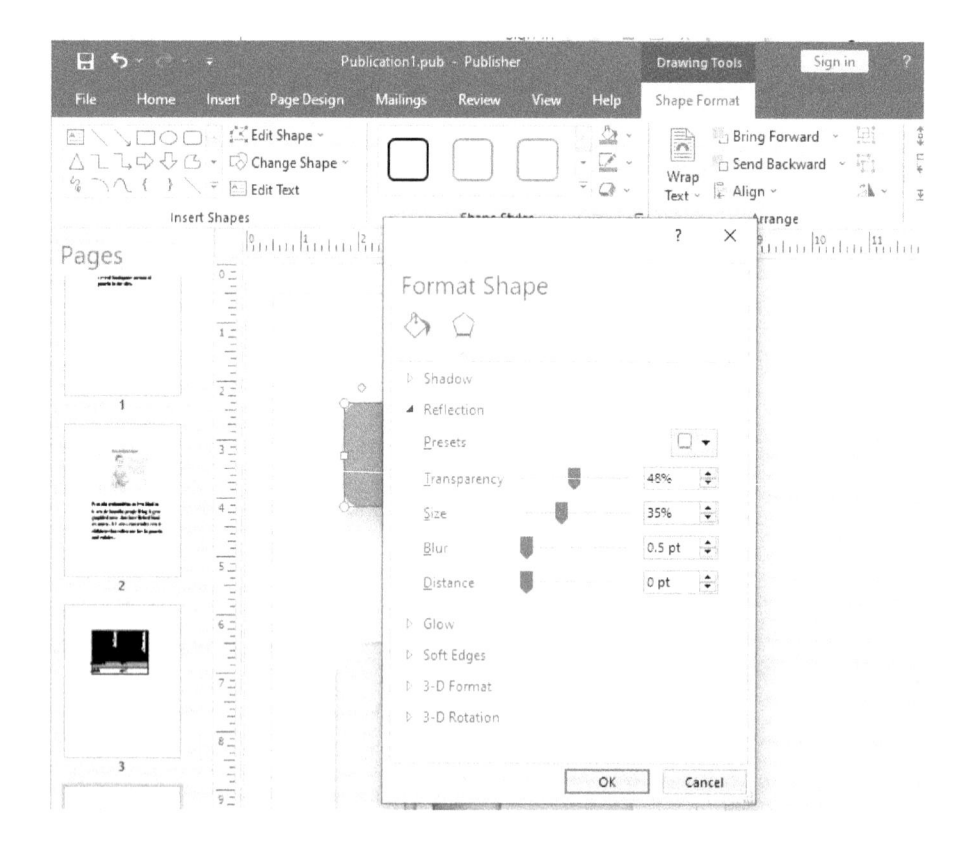

Organize your effect by using the sliders.

Adding Objects Alignment

You can naturally align objects on your page. Heed to the steps beneath to accomplish this.

1. Choose the objects you want to align.
2. Press down the control key on the keyboard while you tick on the images you want to align
3. Select the 'picture tools' format tab
4. and tick 'Arrange'
5. tick align

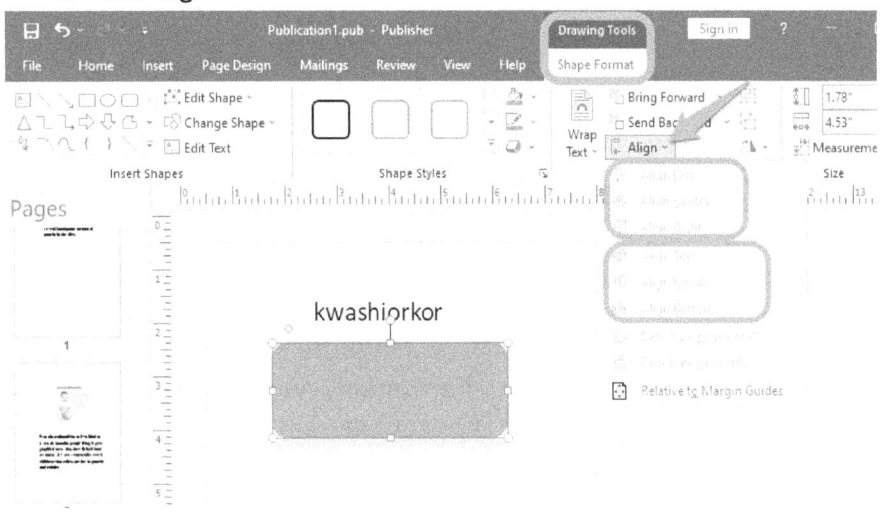

Select a choice from the drop-down menu. Either Align Right, Align Centre, Align Left, Align Top, Align Middle, or Align Bottom.

When you choose Align Left it will align the left side of the objects with the left frame of the leftmost picked object. You can also attempt all other aligns to see what the object would look like.

The Objects Distribution

You can passively distribute several objects equally across your page. To perform this, click all the objects you want to distribute. Long press the control key on the keyboard while you tick on the images you want to distribute. Choose the 'picture tools' format tab and pick 'arrange'. Choose 'align'

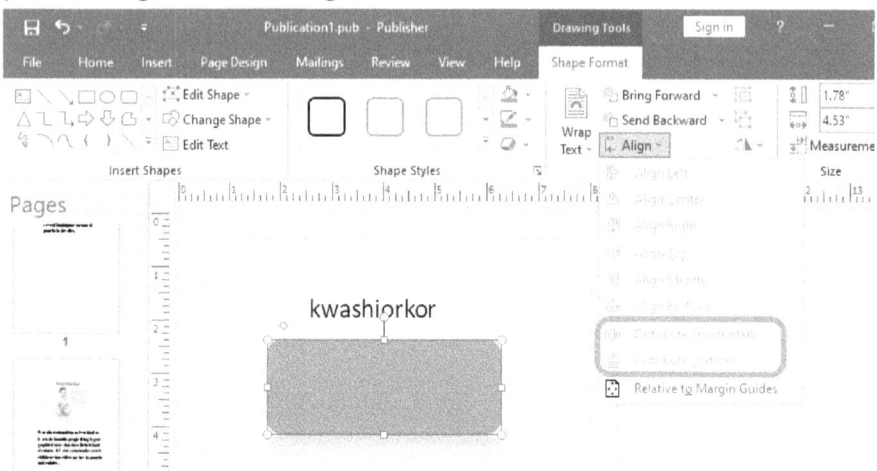

Pick either to distribute vertically or distribute horizontally from the drop-down menu. Distributing horizontally will move the picked objects an equal length apart horizontally all over your selection while distributing vertically will move the picked objects an equal length apart vertically all over your selection.

Objects Grouping Object

You can group many objects into one object for them to stick together. This can be very useful if you have made a graphic containing many shapes and objects so you can rescale and move devoid of having to alter each shape. If you want to do this, tick all the objects you want to group. Long press the control key on the keyboard while you are taping the images.

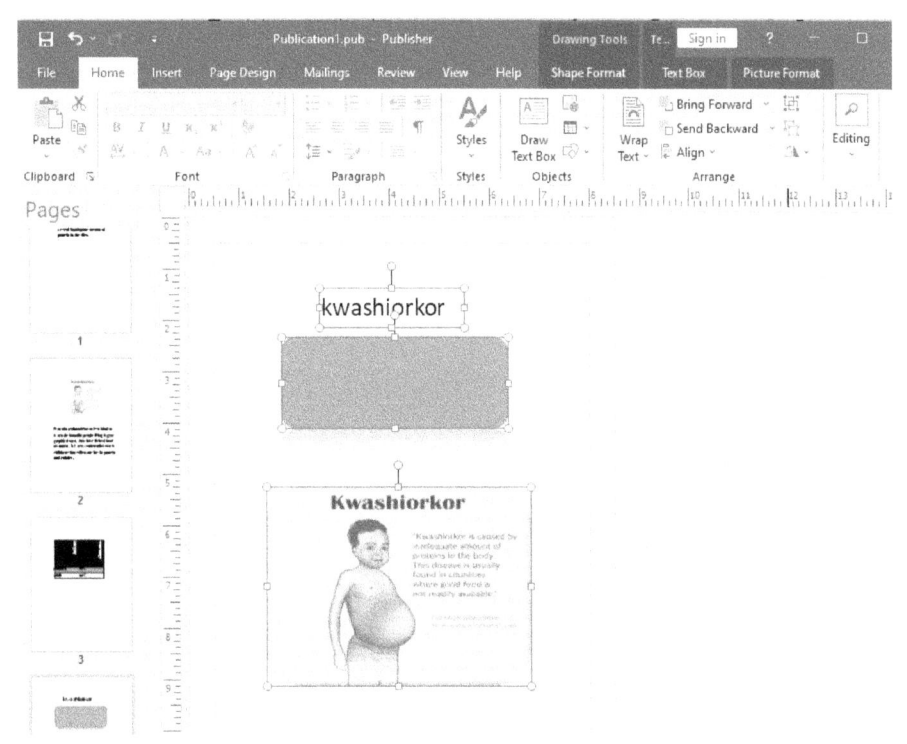

Select the 'picture tools' or 'drawing tools' format tab then tick 'group'.

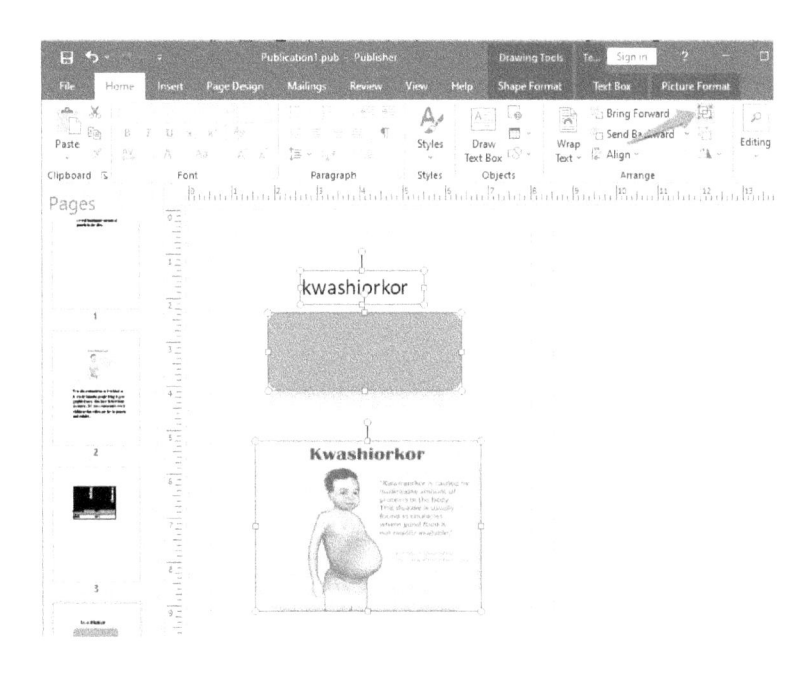

See the outcome below:

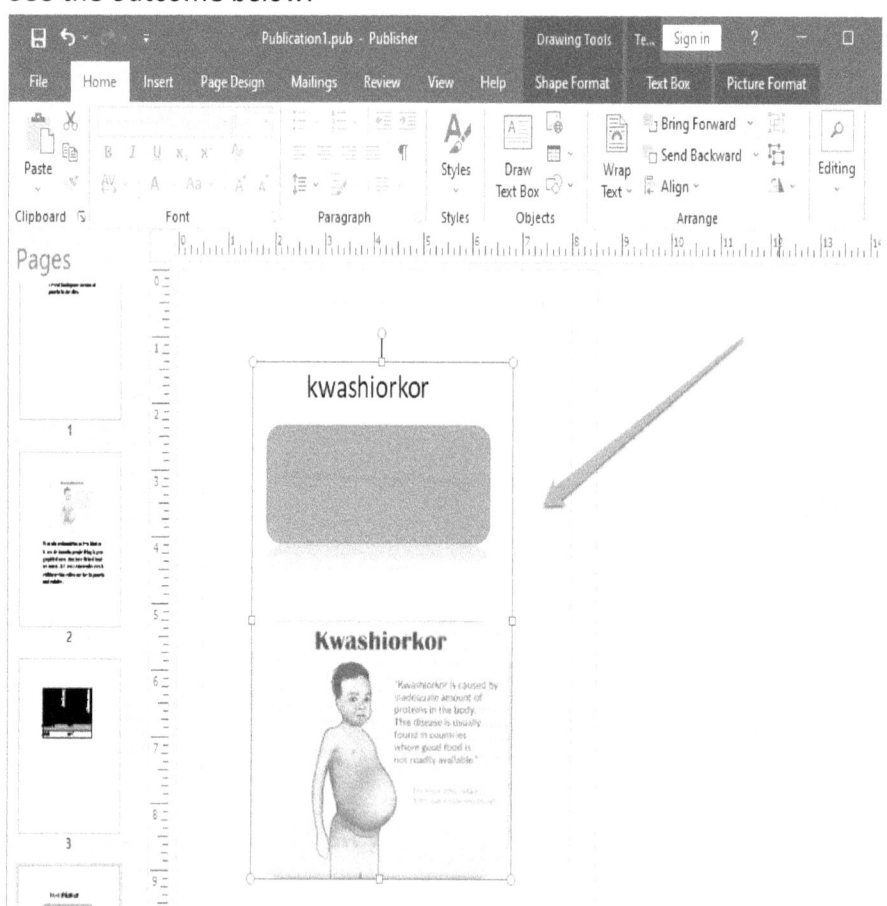

You will be able to easily shift the graphic as a single object. If you wish to ungroup, tick on the object then choose 'ungroup' from the 'drawing tools' or the 'picture tools.

Setting Object Layers

Publications are produced using crystalline layers. Whenever you insert an image, object, shape, or text box, it is going to have a new layer at the topmost. Study this for illustration:

kwashiorkor

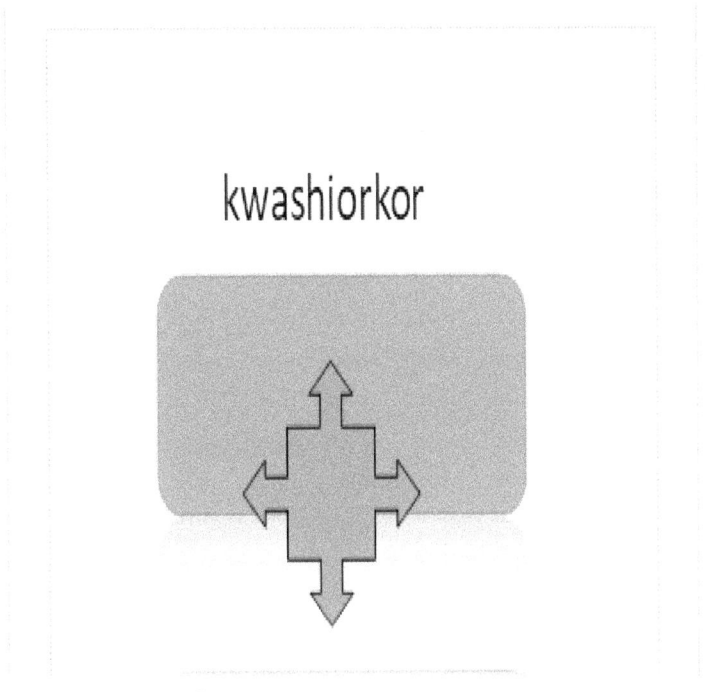

We can have a layer like this:

The Page parts

The publisher has diverse pre-designed building blocks to help you design your page. You can quickly attach sidebars or titles to your page as well as preformatted quotes and stories. Abide by the steps beneath to insert a page part:

1. Tick the insert tab.
2. Tick on-page parts.
3. Choose a template from the drop-down menu.

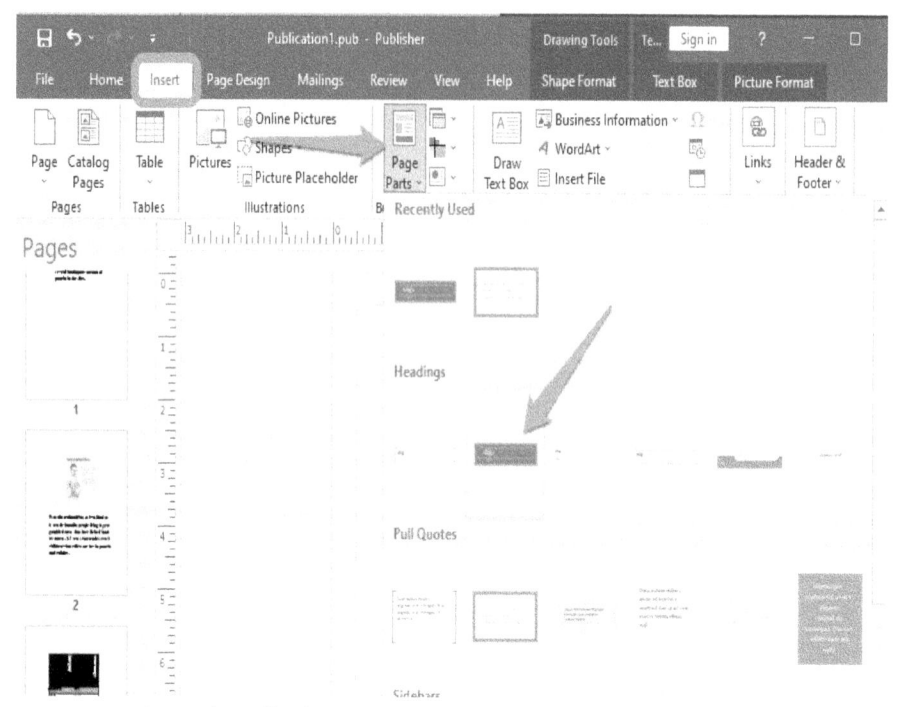

4. Tick and pull the page part into bearings and rescale it if required.

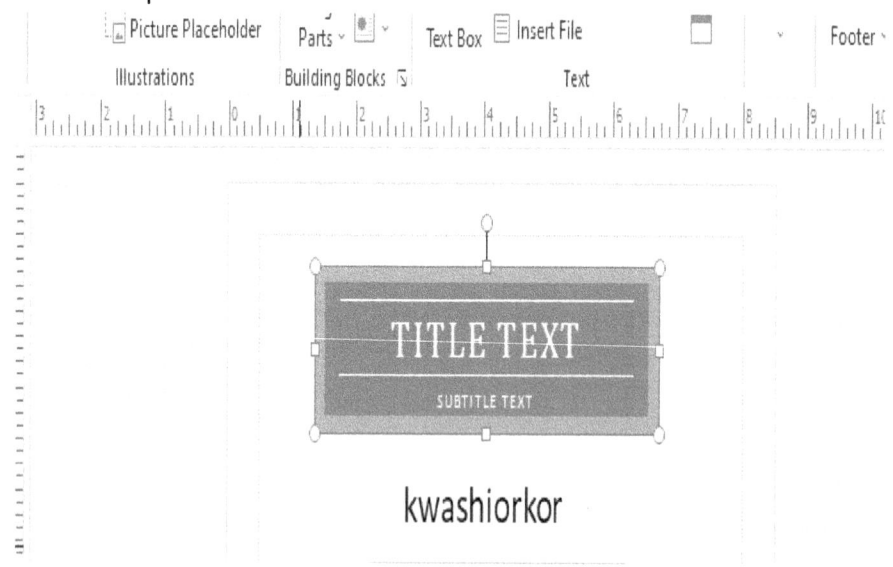

You can type your text in the placeholders.

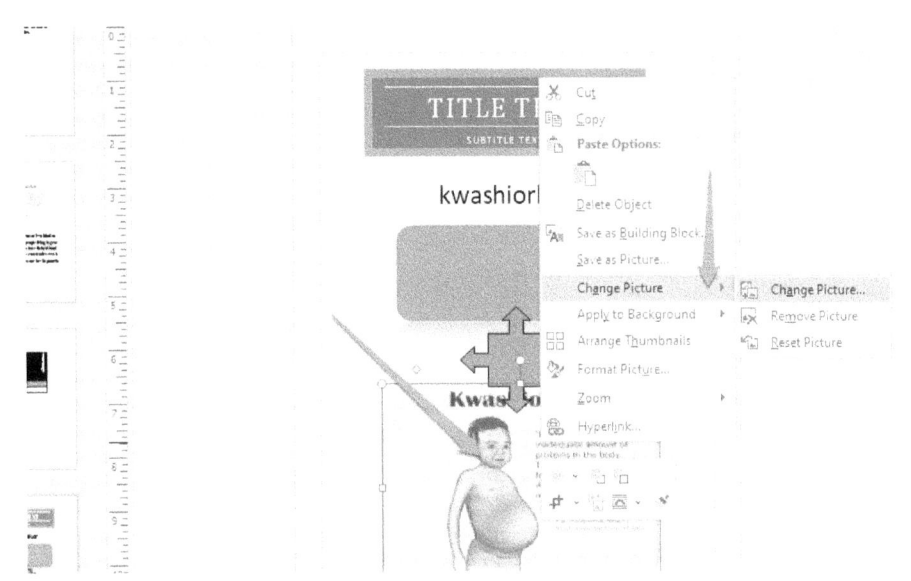

Right-click on the image if there is an image, then go downward to 'change picture' and pick 'change picture' from the slideout.

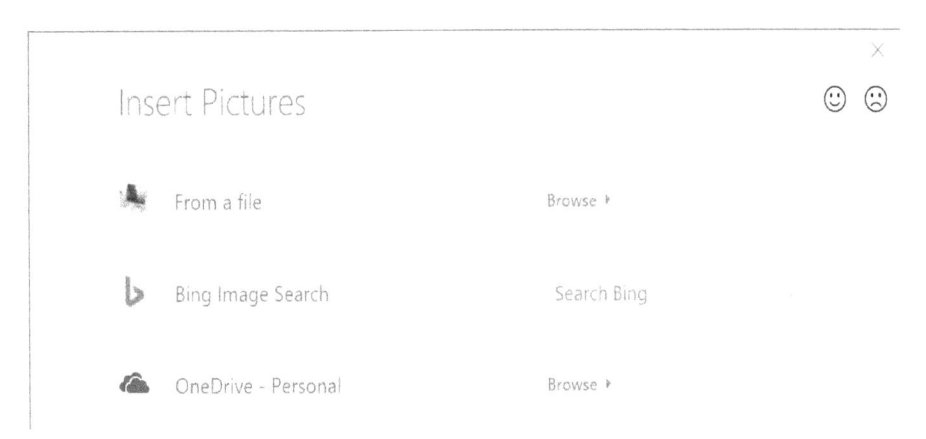

Select where you desire to input your picture, then choose your picture.

If you would like to alter the colors. Tick on the page part, and pick the 'drawing tools' format tab.

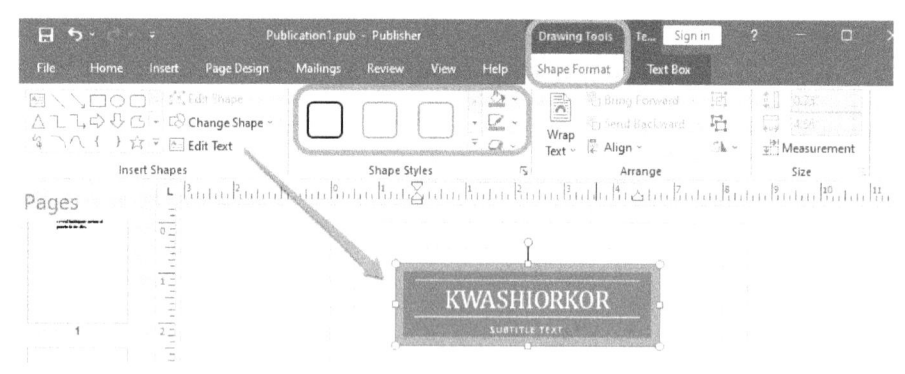

You can apply the shape fill to change the fill color from this place, shape outline to fix the border colors, and shape effects to insert shadows or reflections to the page part. I apply a shape to fill in the image below:

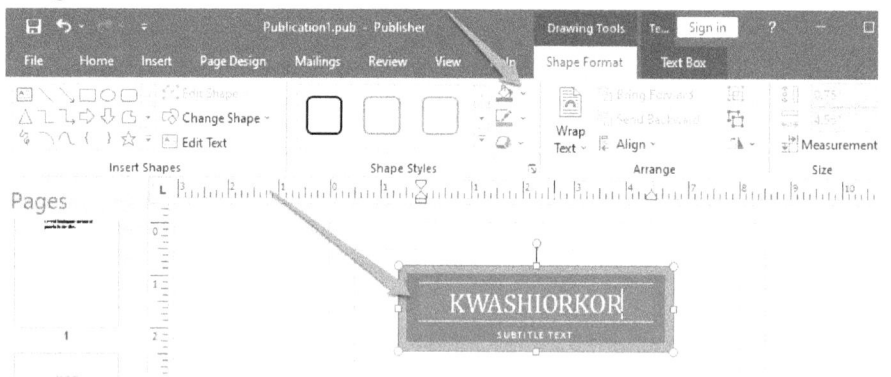

You can also make use of the shape-style programs on this ribbon tab.

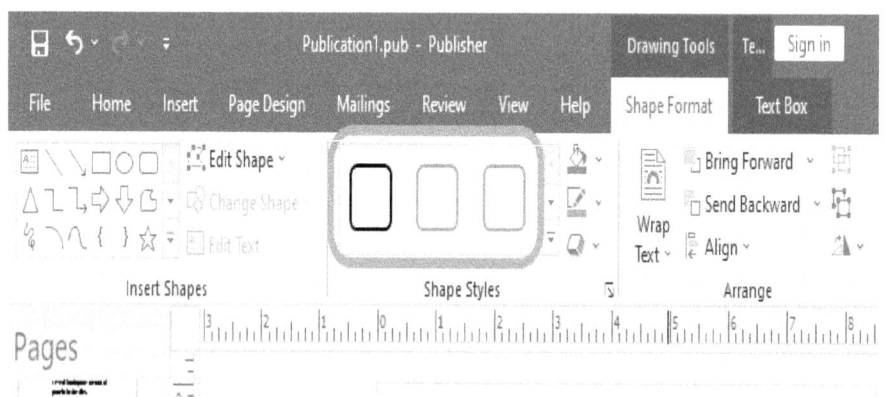

Select one and give it a test.

Including Borders and Accents

You can add borders on your page, text box, or image. You can also insert accents which are tiny decorations that are used to stress other objects. For you to add an accent, tick on the insert tab then choose borders and accents.

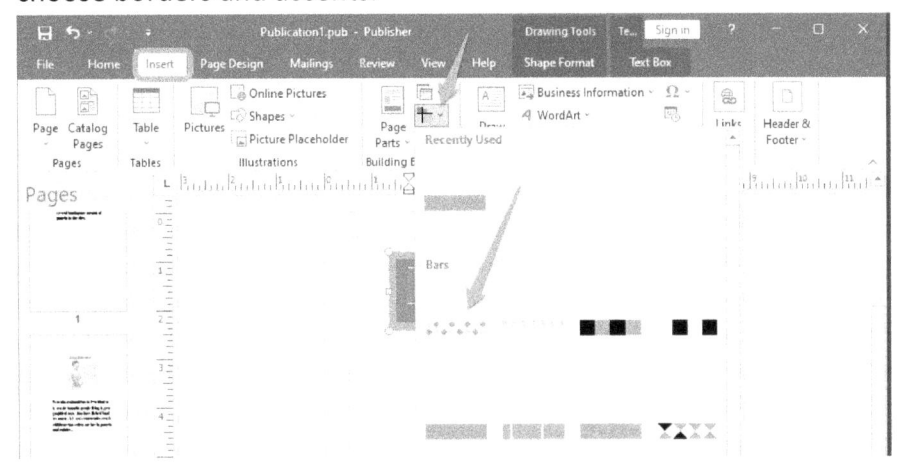

Resize and pull the accent to where you want it to be.

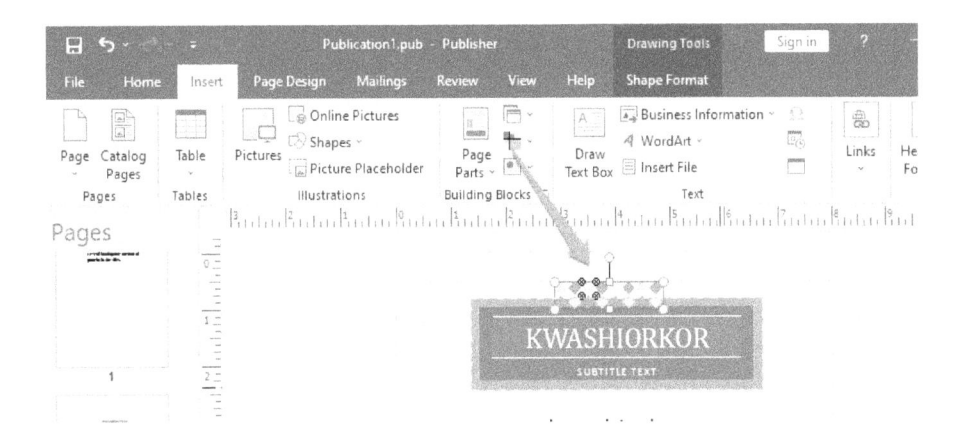

Adding Calendars to Your Publisher

If you want to add a calendar, tick on the insert tab then tap 'calendars' and choose a template from the drop-down menu.

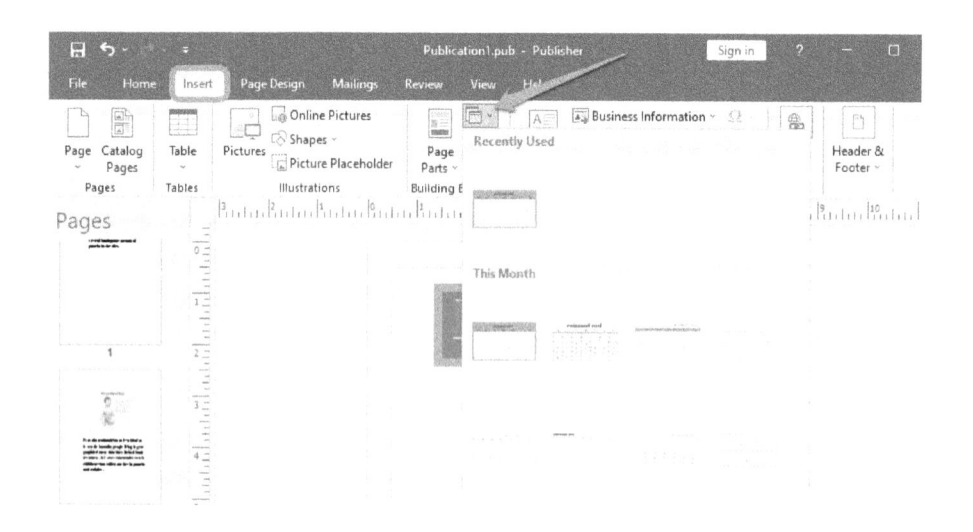

Resize and move your calendar into place.

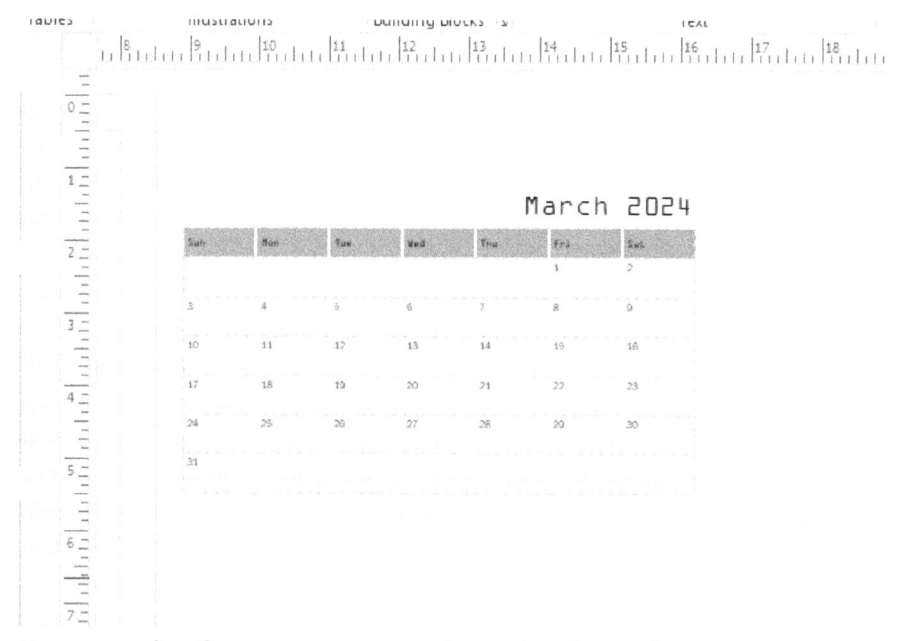

For example, if you want to attach a calendar with an exact month, choose 'more calendar' from the calendar drop-down menu.

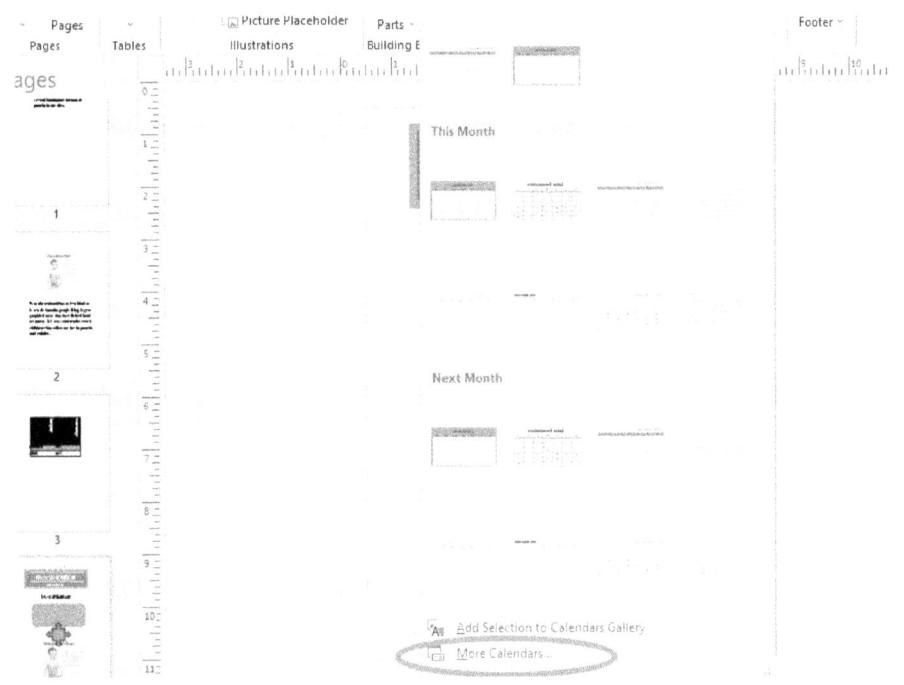

Select a blueprint or format, then put the month and the year into the box on the right-hand side. Tick 'insert' when you are done.

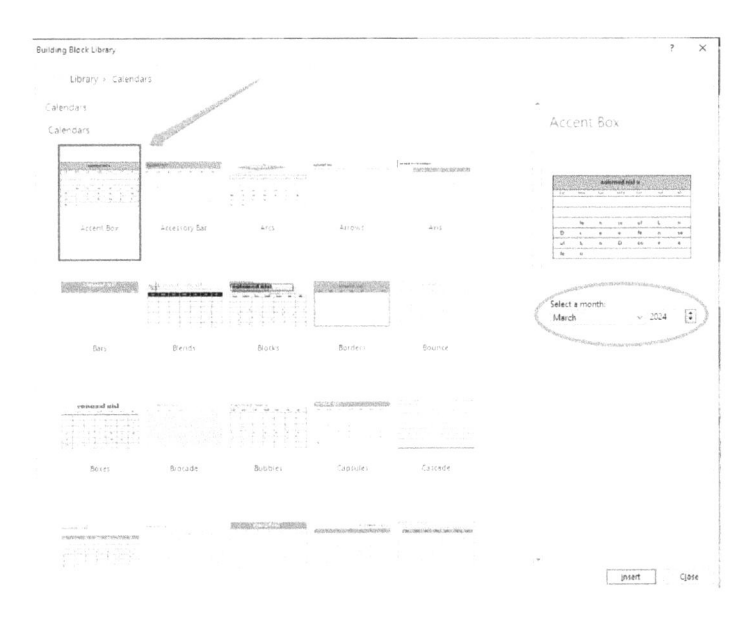

Producing Advertisements

You can swiftly produce free offers, ads, attention grabbers, and coupons. To perform this you have to abide by the steps beneath

1. Tick on the Insert tab.
2. Choose 'advertisements' then select a format from the drop-down menu.
3. For you to be able to view all the ads format tick on 'more advertisements' at the bottom.

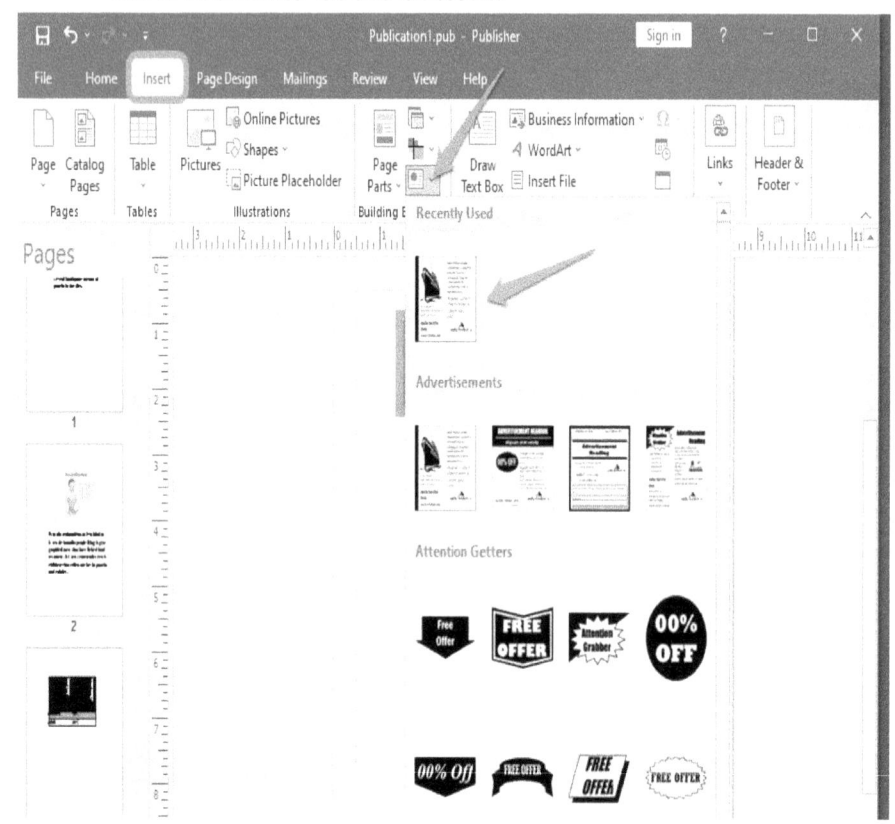

Rescale and move the ad into position on your page.

Put your details into the text boxes.

If you want to alter any images, right-click on the image, then pick 'change image' from the slideout, then select where you want to put in your picture, and then choose your picture.

Inserting WordArt

WordArt is useful for making headings and eye-catching text. To insert WordArt, tick on the 'insert' tab then choose 'WordArt'. Select a style from the drop-down menu.

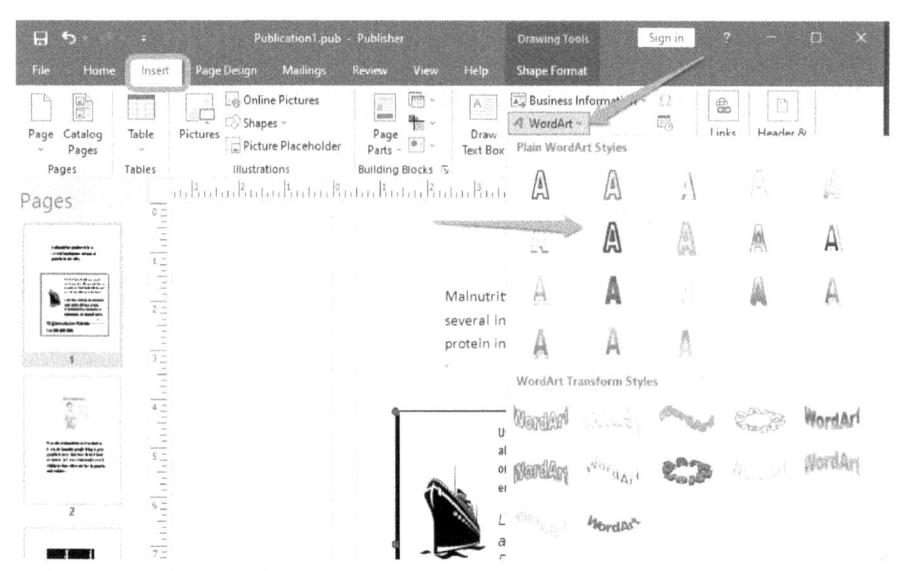

Select your font and size then put in your WordArt text.

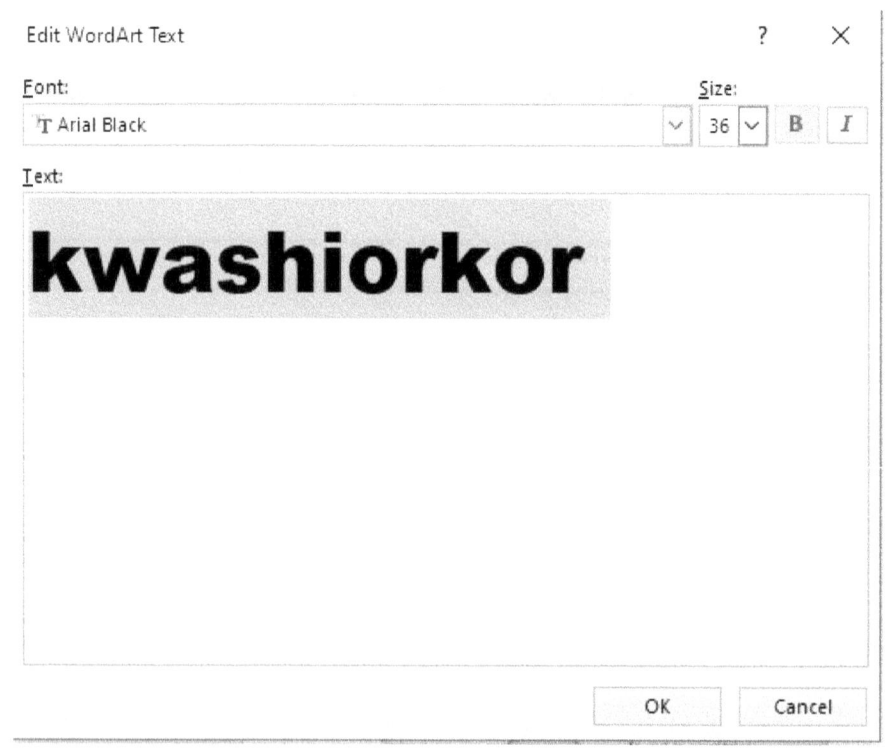

Tick 'ok'

You can alter the style of the text by using the sets up from the WordArt tools format tab,

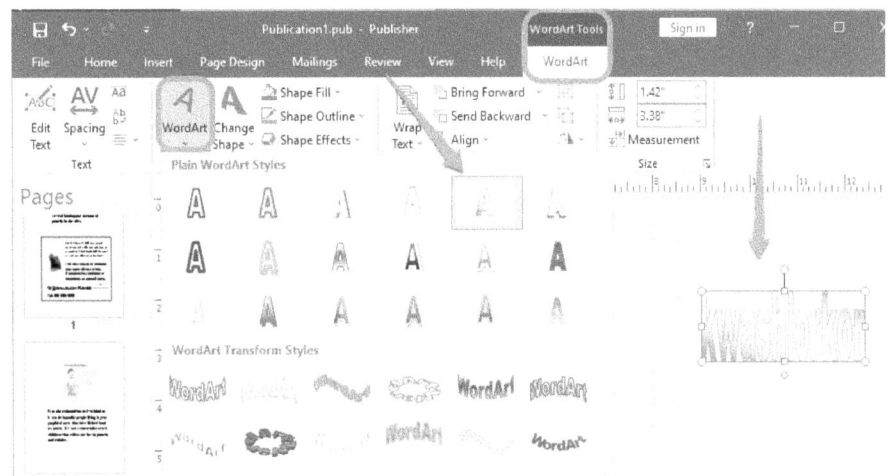

Insert a reflection or shadow effect making use of 'shape effects'.

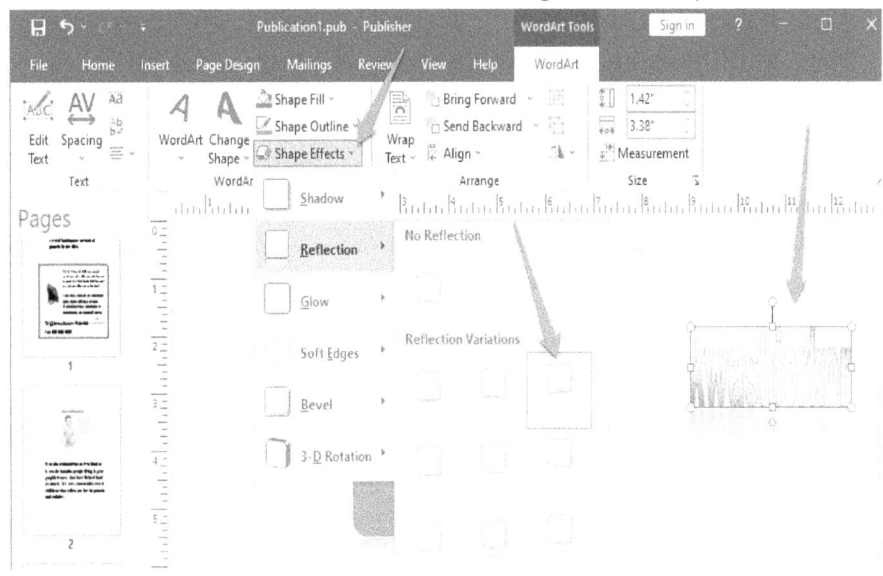

By making use of the 'fill color' you can change the color.

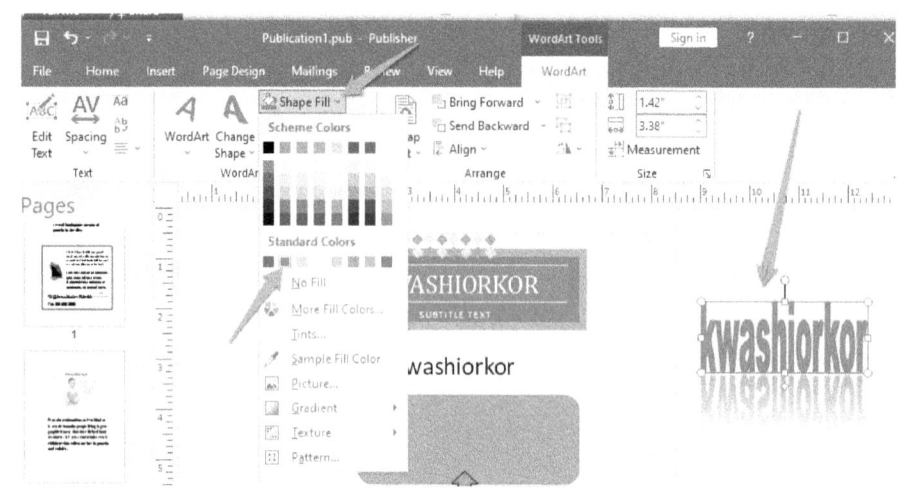

Modify the border of the text using 'shape outline'.

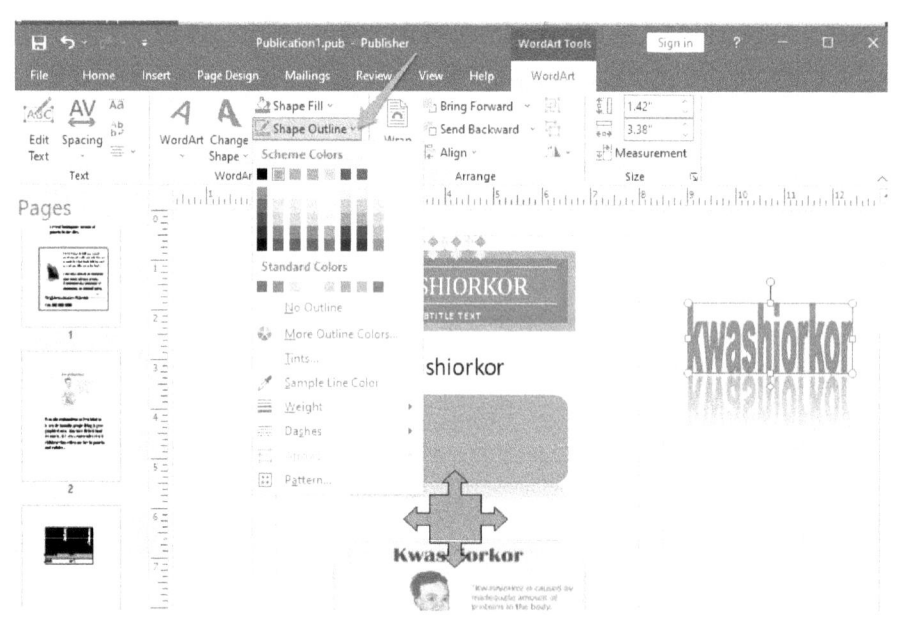

If you want to alter the shape of the text. Tick 'change shape'. Select a shape from the drop-down menu.

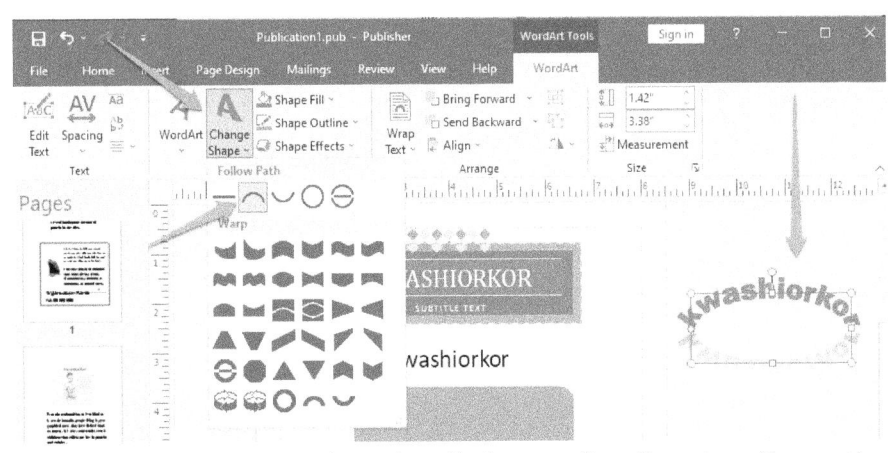

To refine the shape, tick and pull the small yellow handle on the WordArt.

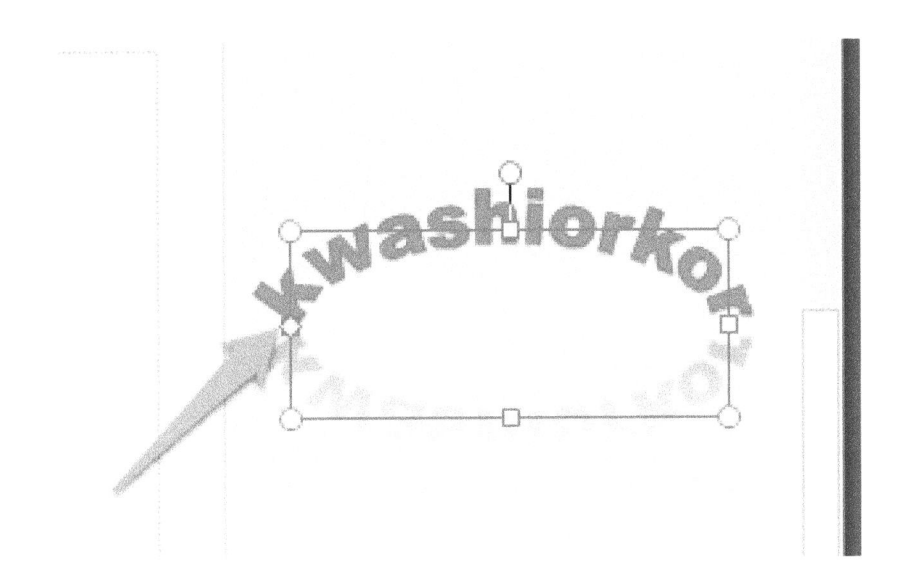

Use the rescale handles to resize your WordArt, and make use of the rotate handle to turn your WordArt.

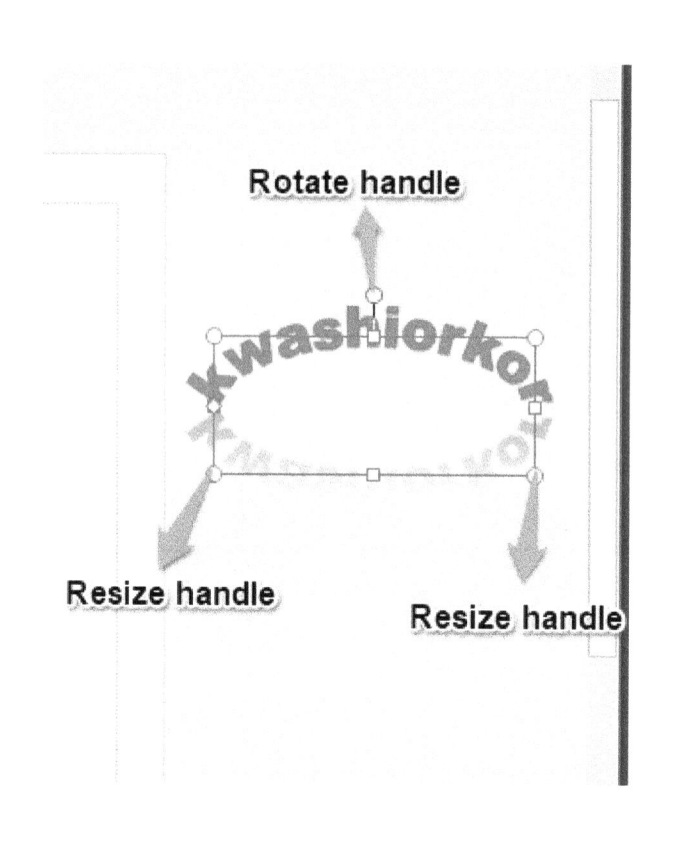

Chapter Five
Producing Mail Merge

Under this section, we shall be focusing on producing a mail merge to produce addressed envelopes and invites using a publisher.

Producing Mail Marge Envelopes

If you have many recipients, producing an envelope for each of them can be time-consuming. This is why mail merge is useful. To accomplish this, you need to open an envelope pattern or produce one. Tap 'new' on the start-up screen, tick on 'built-in' then scroll down and pick 'envelope'.

Scroll down to 'blank sizes' and select the size of the envelope you will be using. Choose 'create'.

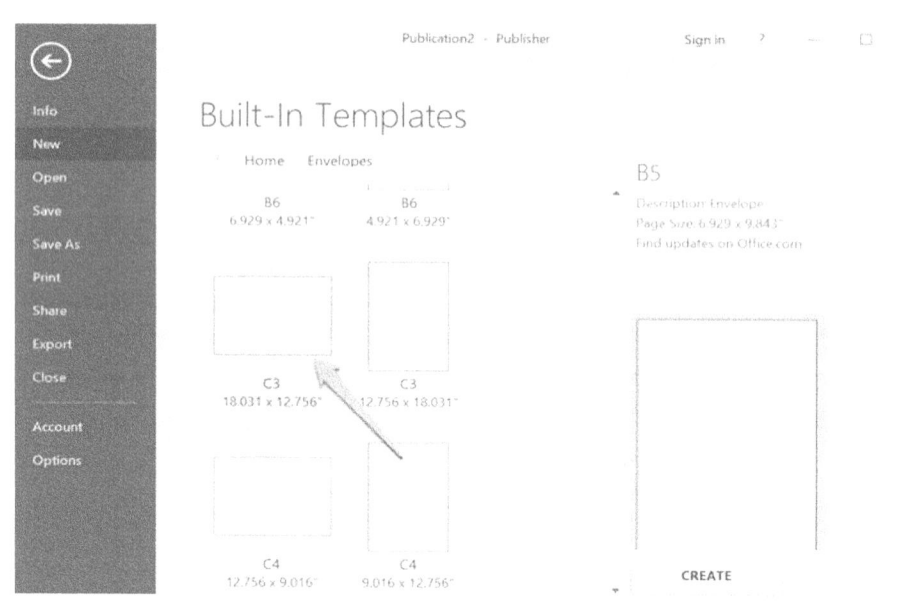

What you will need next is a data source and it is usually a list of names and addresses. The top position to save names and addresses is in an Excel spreadsheet. I have one of my clients list that I saved in an Excel spreadsheet, so in this illustration, I will make use of it. You can also make use of the same method if you use your Outlook contacts.

To select a data source, go to your mailings tab and tick 'select recipients'.

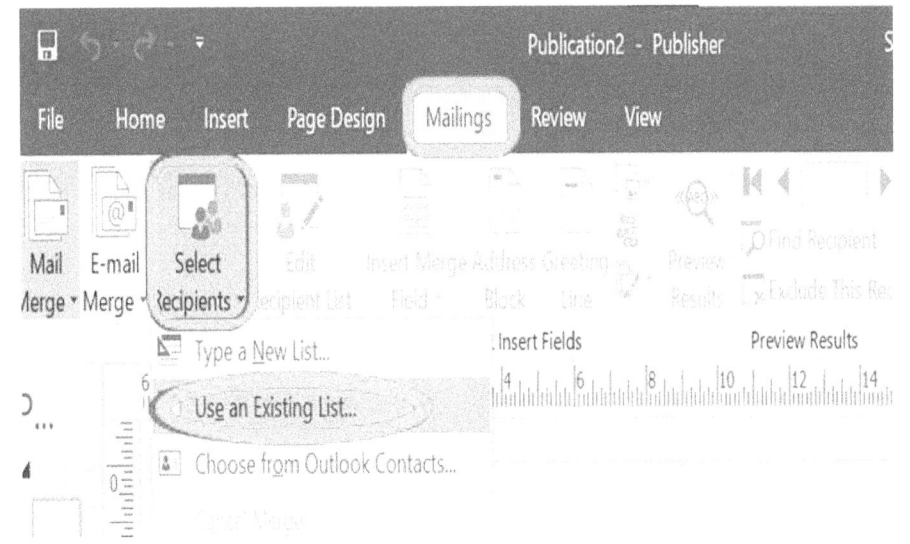

From the drop-down menu, tick 'use an existing list…'.

Look for your data source from the dialog box that appears, I will pick my Excel spreadsheet. Mail Merge Data1

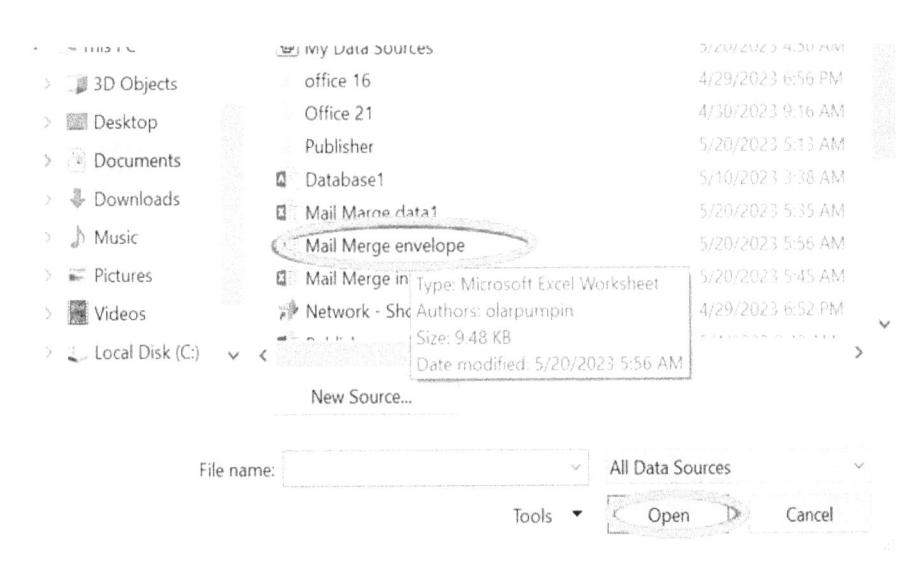

Tick 'open'

Then tick 'ok' on the next two dialog boxes that come up.

Select Table

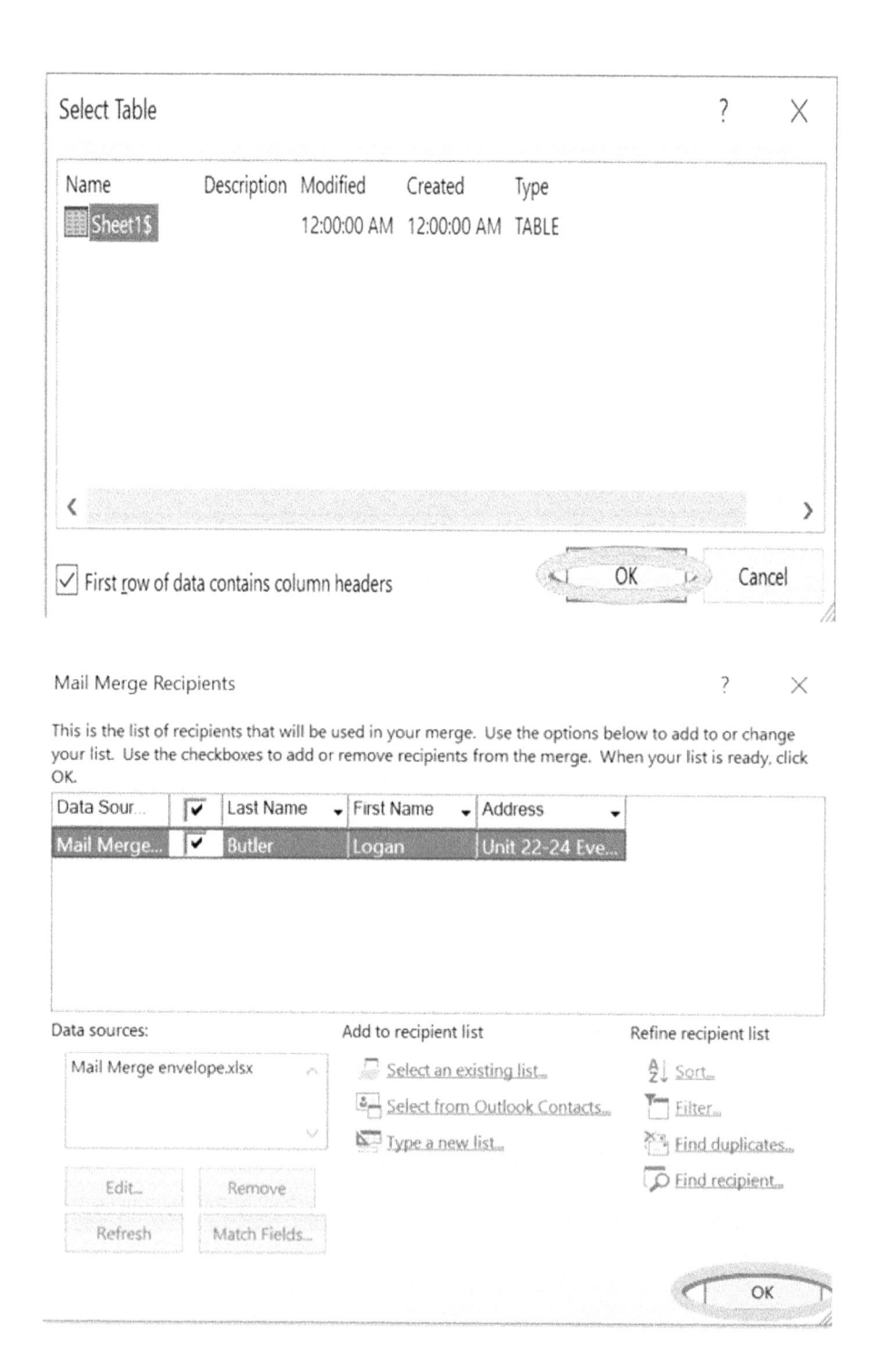

Name	Description	Modified	Created	Type
Sheet1$		12:00:00 AM	12:00:00 AM	TABLE

☑ First row of data contains column headers   OK   Cancel

Mail Merge Recipients

This is the list of recipients that will be used in your merge. Use the options below to add to or change your list. Use the checkboxes to add or remove recipients from the merge. When your list is ready, click OK.

Data Sour...	☑	Last Name	First Name	Address
Mail Merge...	☑	Butler	Logan	Unit 22-24 Eve...

Data sources:
Mail Merge envelope.xlsx

Edit...   Remove
Refresh   Match Fields...

Add to recipient list
- Select an existing list...
- Select from Outlook Contacts...
- Type a new list...

Refine recipient list
- Sort...
- Filter...
- Find duplicates...
- Find recipient...

OK

To produce your envelopes, pick 'address block' from the mailings tab, to attach the addresses from your contacts data source.

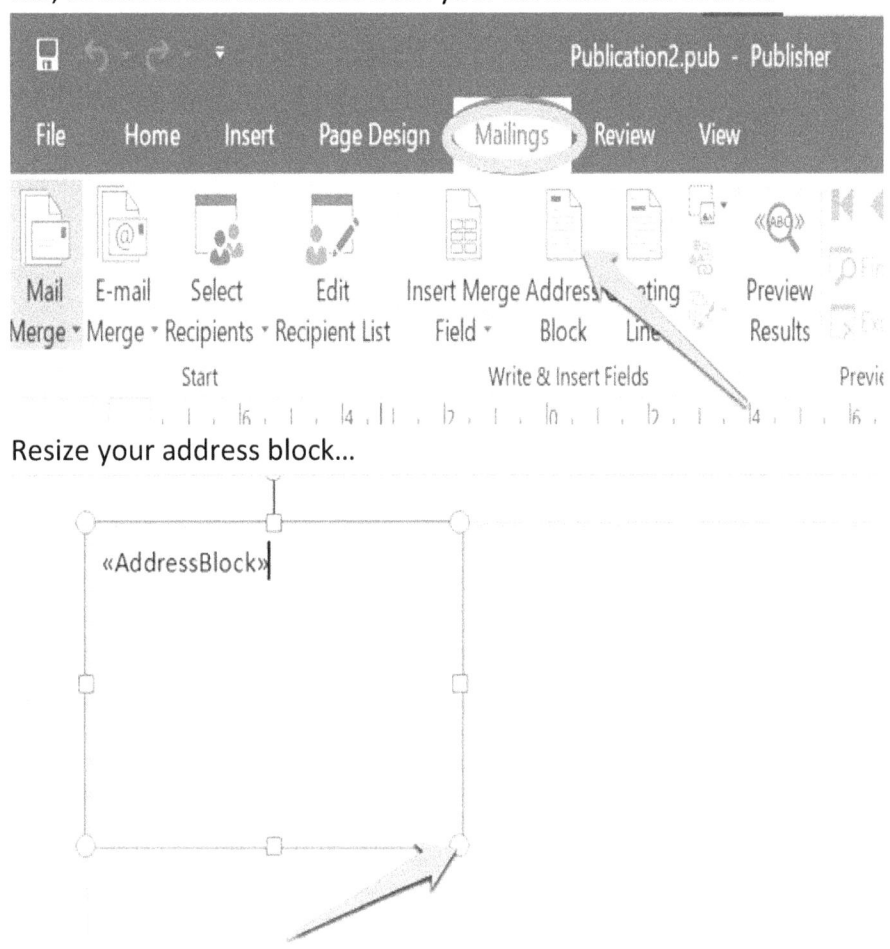

Resize your address block...

To exhibit your envelopes, from the Mailings tab choose 'preview results'. By using the next/previous record icons, you can turn over through the envelopes.

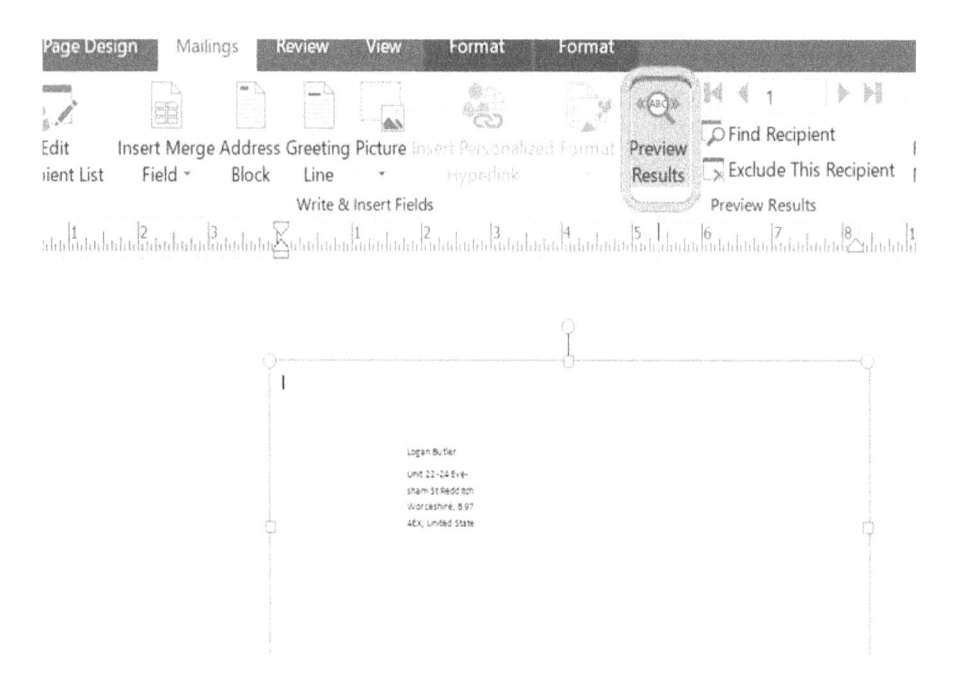

To accomplish your work to the end, from the Mailings tab tick 'finish and merge'. From the drop-down menu, choose 'print documents' to send a large of it to the printer, to be sure that you have already loaded your envelopes into your printer's paper tray.

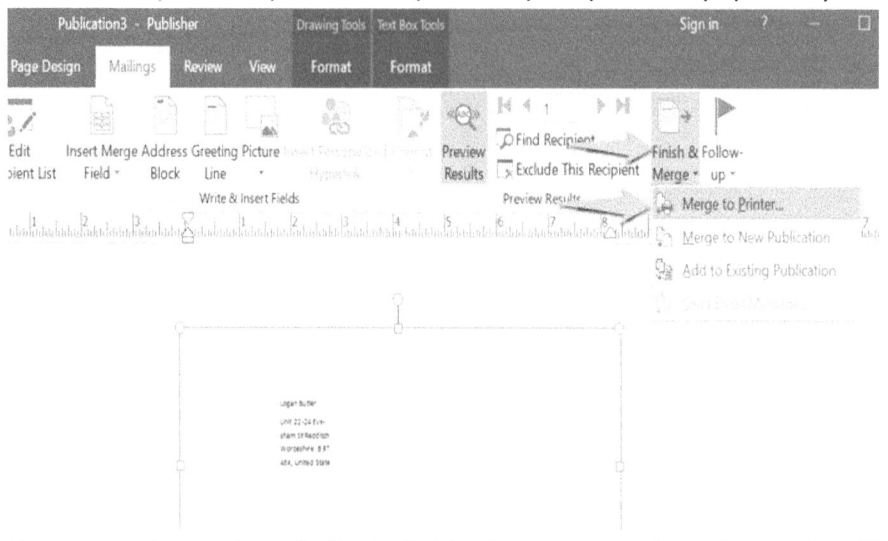

You can also select 'edit individual documents' and Word will produce a document with all your envelopes set to print. This is useful if you only want to print certain addresses or make some changes.

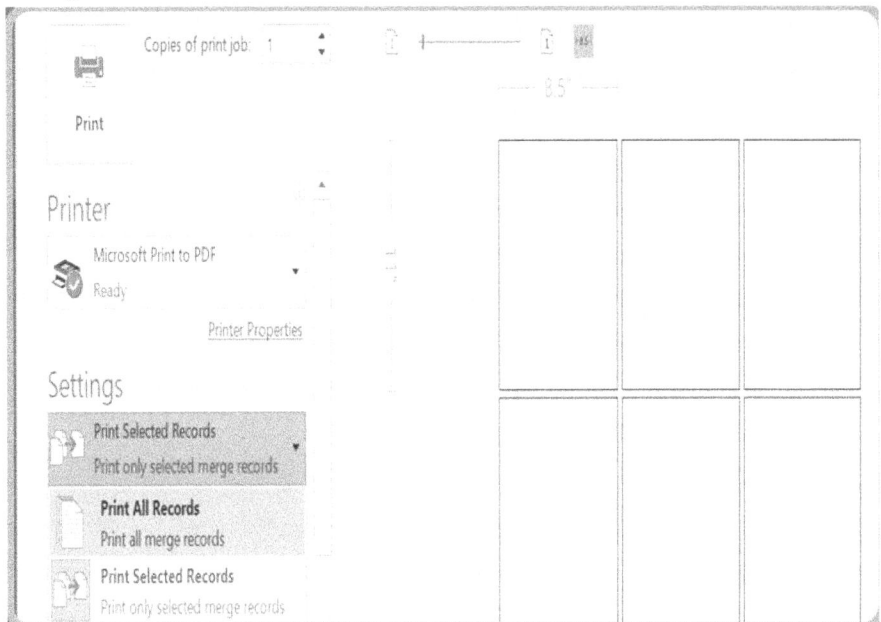

Select 'print all records' from the dialog box that comes up.

Producing Mail Merge Invitation

As our envelopes have been printed, there's a need for us to create our party invitation. To produce this, open a pattern. Tick 'new' on the publisher's start screen, and type in the publication pattern you want in the search area. I will be putting a birthday party in the search area.

Then double-tap on the pattern you desire.

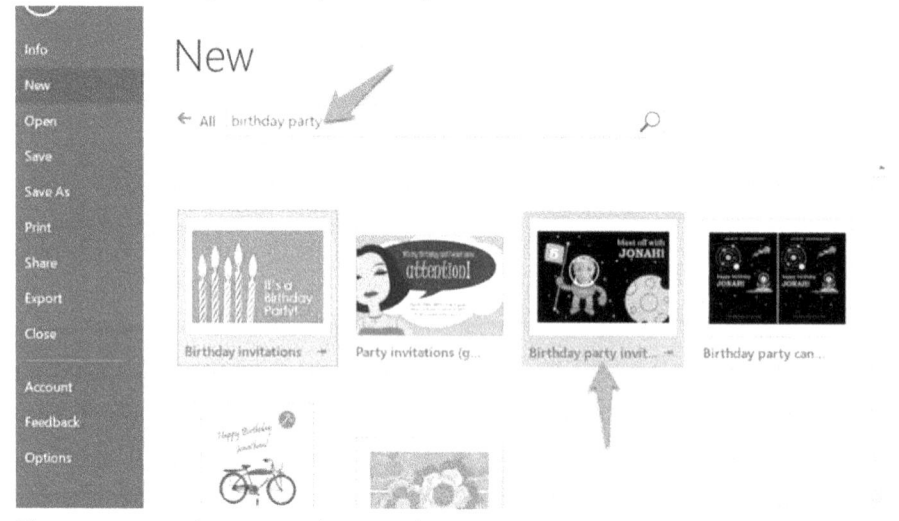

The next step is to attach your data source. To add your data source, tick on your mailings tab and pick 'select recipients'. Then choose 'use an existing list' from the drop-down list.

Then pick your data file.

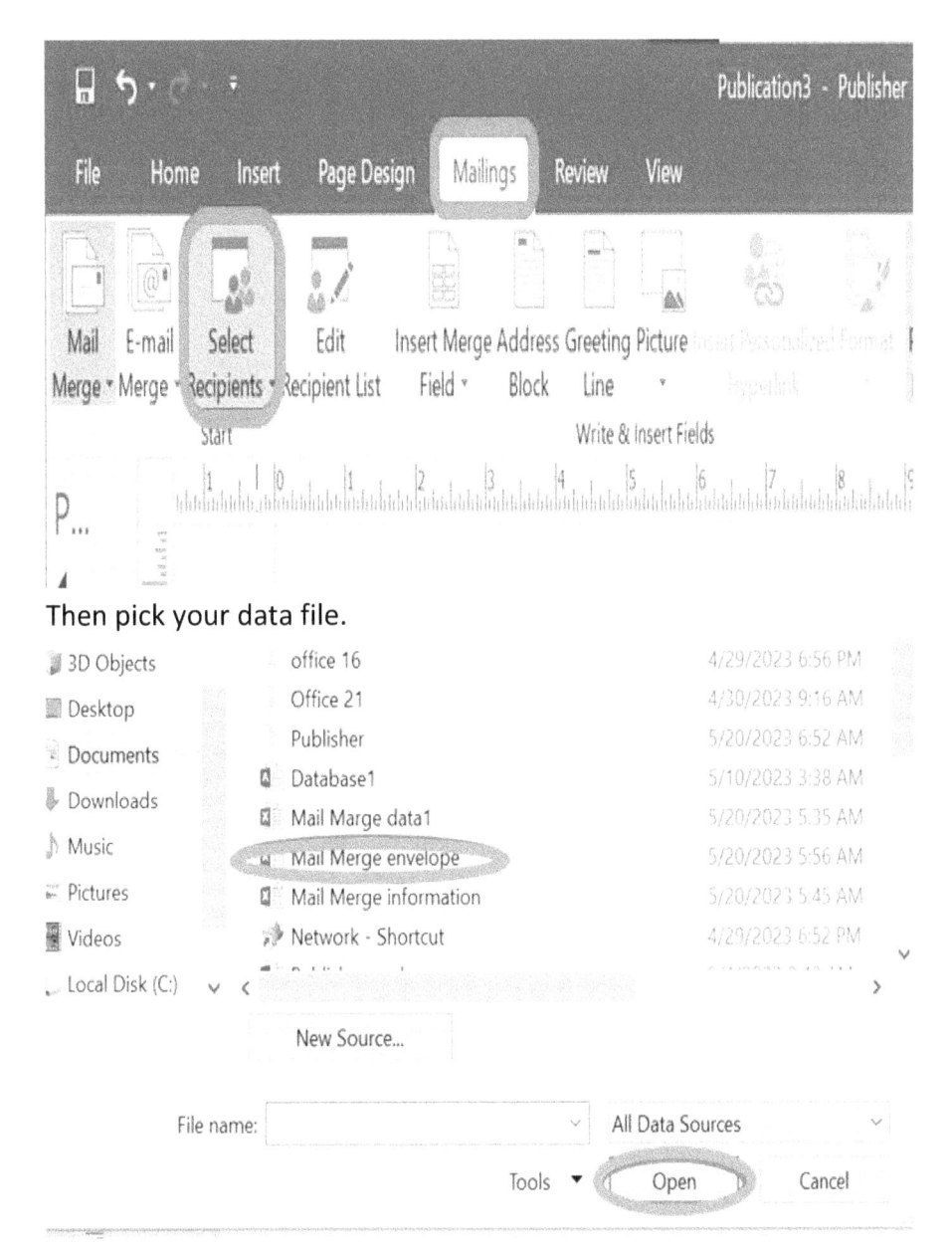

Tick open on the dialog box. We can start to attach names now. Choose 'insert merge field', from the mailings tab. And from the drop-down pick 'first name', tick 'insert merge field', and pick 'last name'.

111

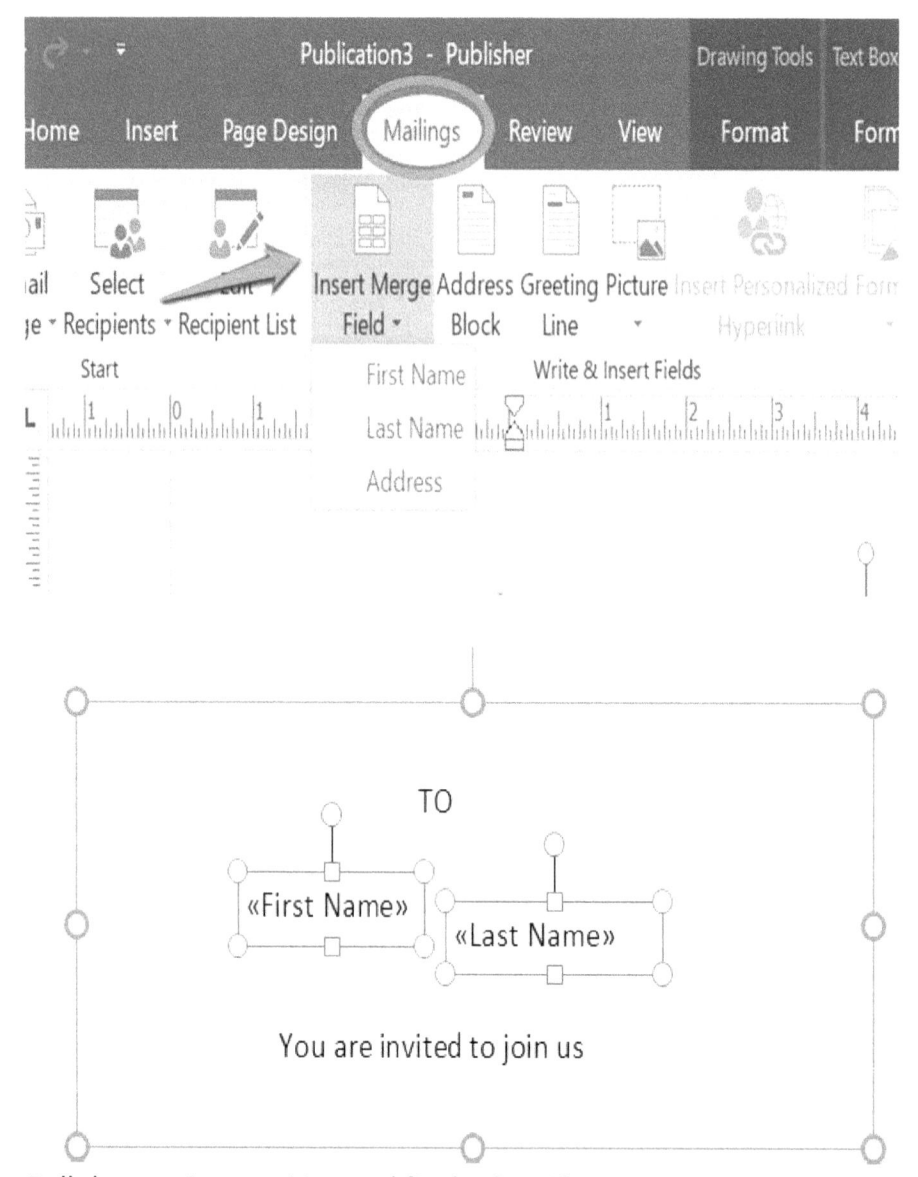

Pull the text into position and fix the font if it is necessary.

Once you have entered all the fields, from the mailings tab choose 'preview results'. You will get something like this (an individualized invitation for each name):

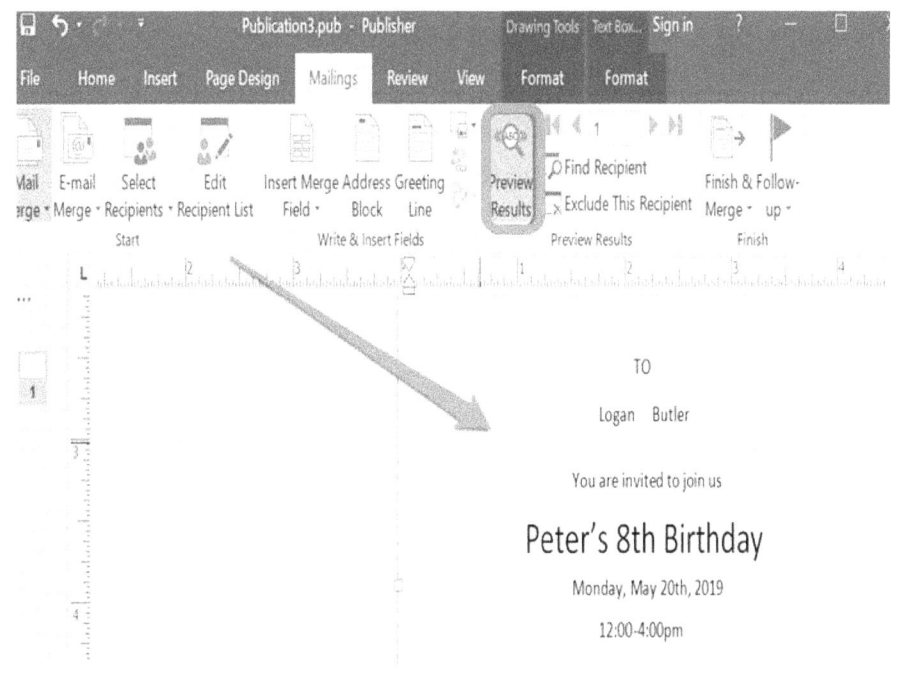

To finalize, from the mailings tab, tick 'finish & merge'

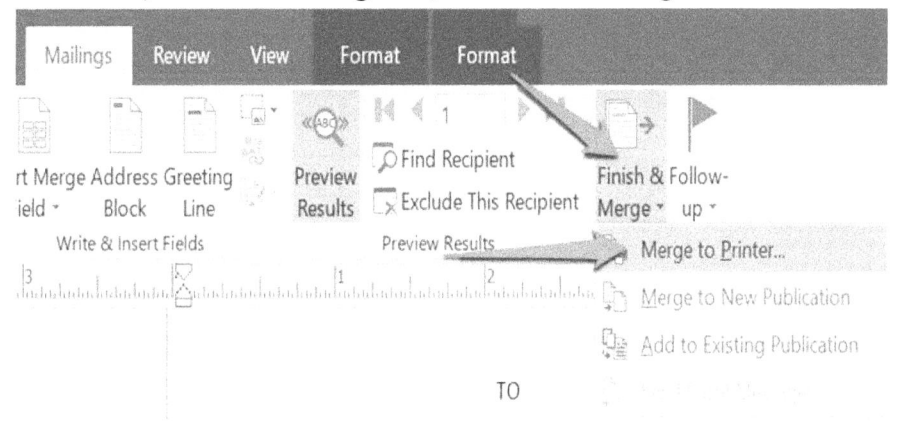

Choose 'print document' to send all the letters to the printer.

Making Use of Pre-designed Templates

In this section, we shall be taking a look at several different pre-designed templates that come with the publisher, also building a template from the beginning.

Discovering a Pre-designed Template

When you activate the publisher, you will observe a screen consisting of thumbnails of various templates that are accessible. To find the template, tick 'new' on the left-hand side.

The best way to find templates is to look for them.

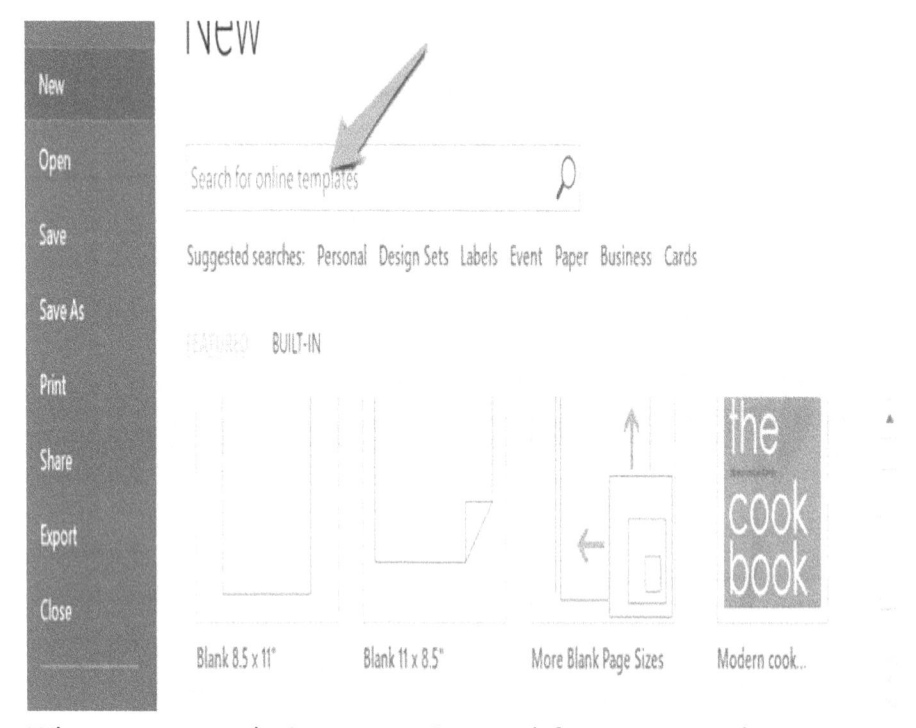

Why not try producing a greeting card for someone that you are familiar with?

Open publisher, choose 'new' on the left-hand side, then type... **Birthday card** in the search area

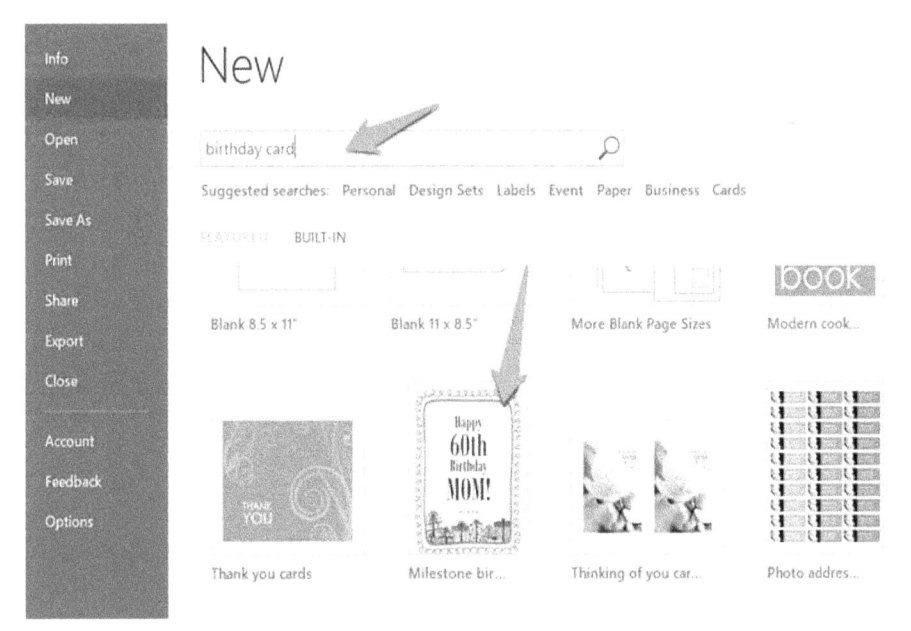

Select a template you can use from the search results. Why not try a lovely Birthday card?

Double-tap on the template thumbnail.

The photo or text can be altered.

What you just have to do is tick on the text and put in your own.

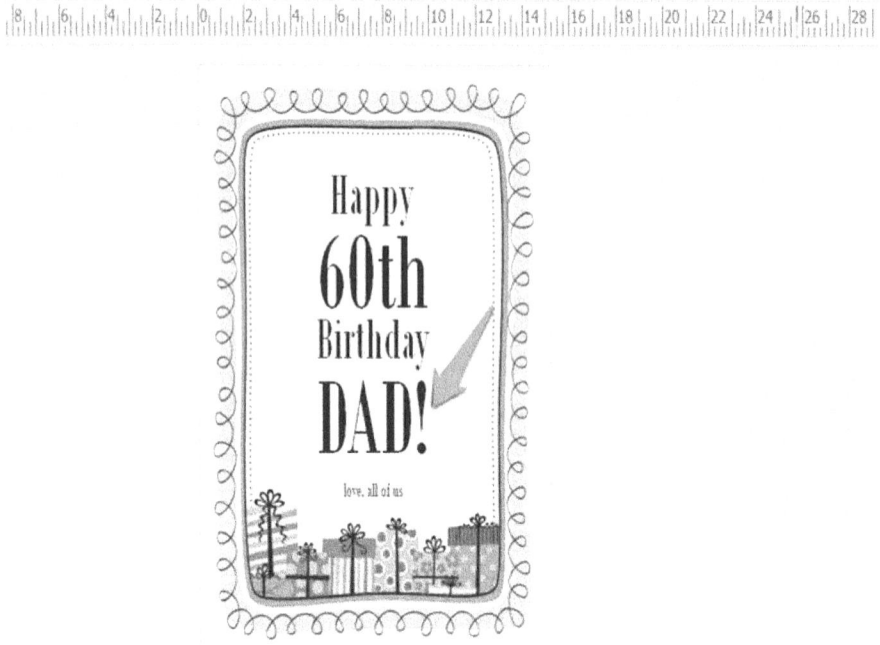

Producing Your Template

If you have produced your style, e.g. fonts, heading sizes, and layouts, you can save this as a template, so you can produce new documents in the same style.

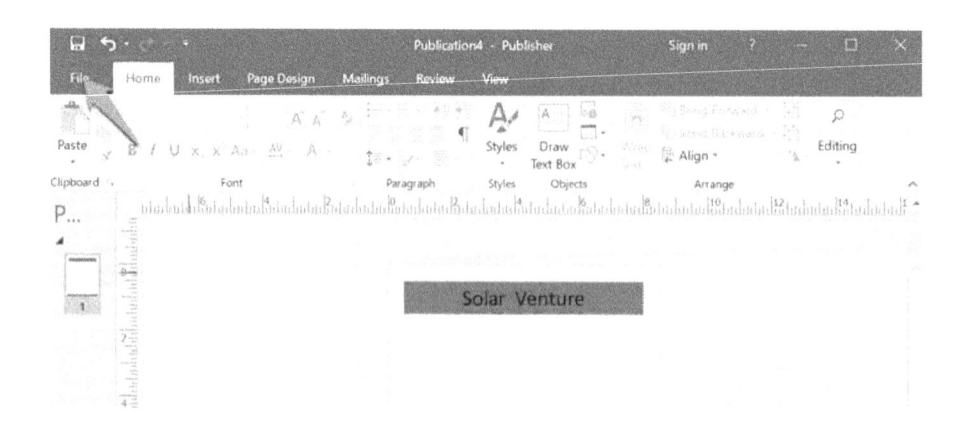

To save your publication as a template, choose 'file' on the top left. Choose 'save as' from the backstage menu. Select your 'OneDrive' folder. From the popup 'save as' dialog box, move down to 'save as type'. Change this to 'publisher template', then tick 'save'. To create a new file using the way, from the publisher start screen, tick 'new'. Scroll down and select 'personal'. Double-tap your pattern. You can now start to put in your text. For you to store it as a new publication, tick 'file' on the top left of the screen. Choose 'save as. Select a folder to store your document in, and give the file a meaning.

Chapter Six
Operating Publication

In this section, we will examine the following: saving your work, printing, page setup, and page masters.

To store your work, tick on the **File** at the top left-hand side of the screen.

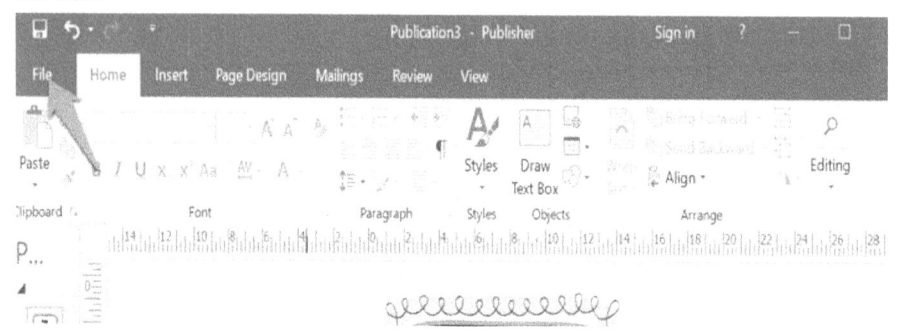

Choose 'save as' on the left-hand side. You will need to let the publisher know where to store the document, in the save as screen. You need to double-tap on **This PC**, then choose where you wish to keep your publication from the dialog box (e.g. in 'document').

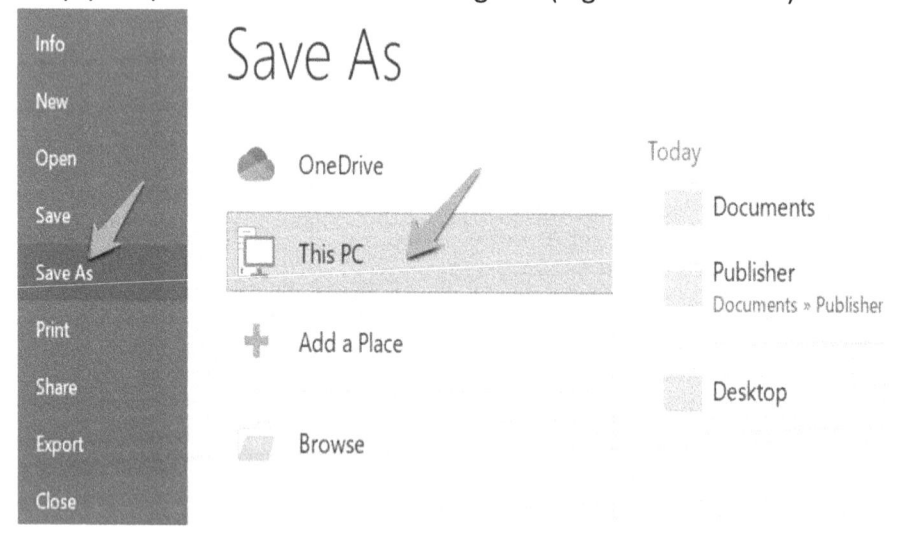

Then you have to give your file a name, in this case, 'Birthday card'. Choose 'save'

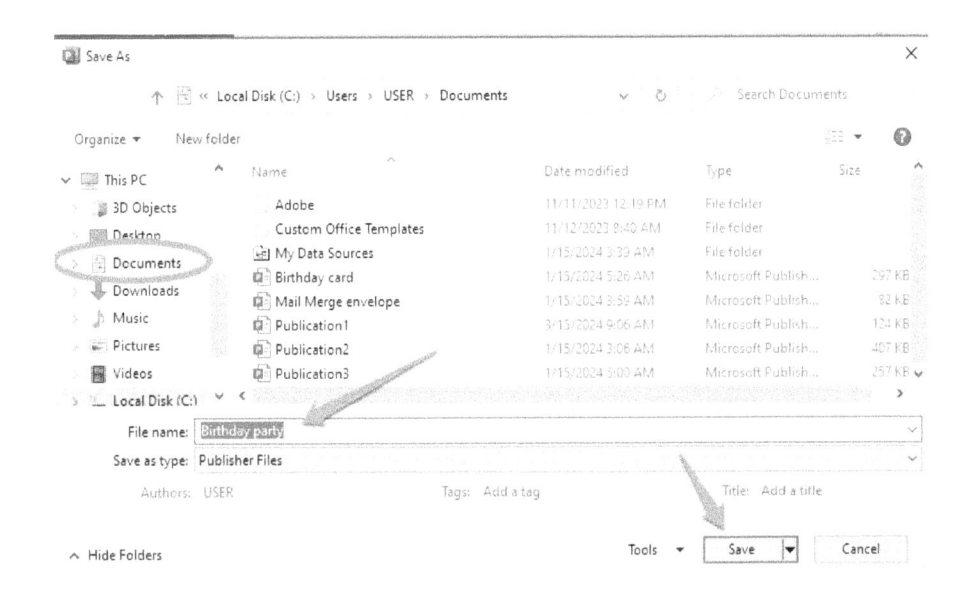

Storing your Publication in a Different Format

Sometimes you will want to store a document in a different format. This can be useful if you are moving a document to another person that might not have Microsoft Office installed or that might not be using Windows.

Publisher allows you to save your document in various formats. A common example is storing files as PDFs, which is a mobile format that can be read on any type of phone, tablet, or computer, phone in the absence of Microsoft Publisher installed.

With your document open, choose the **file** on the top left of the screen. Select 'save as' from the list on the left-hand side.

119

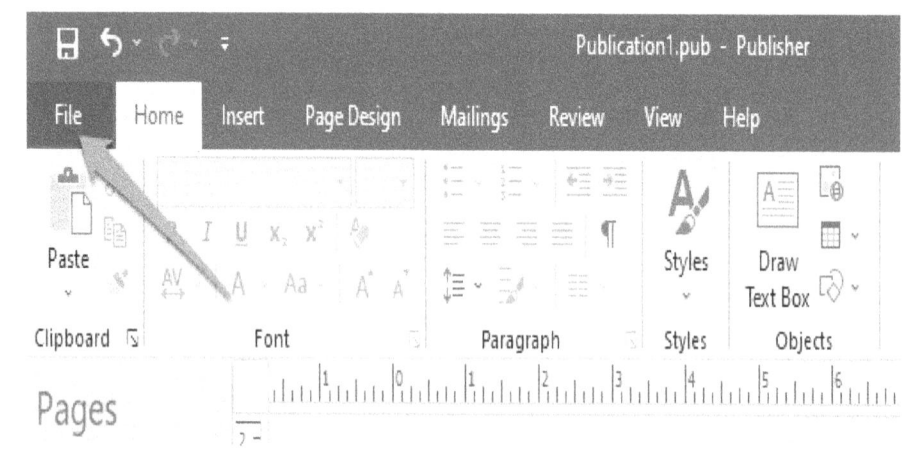

Double-tap 'This PC', and pick the folder you want to save your work into. Eg 'documents.

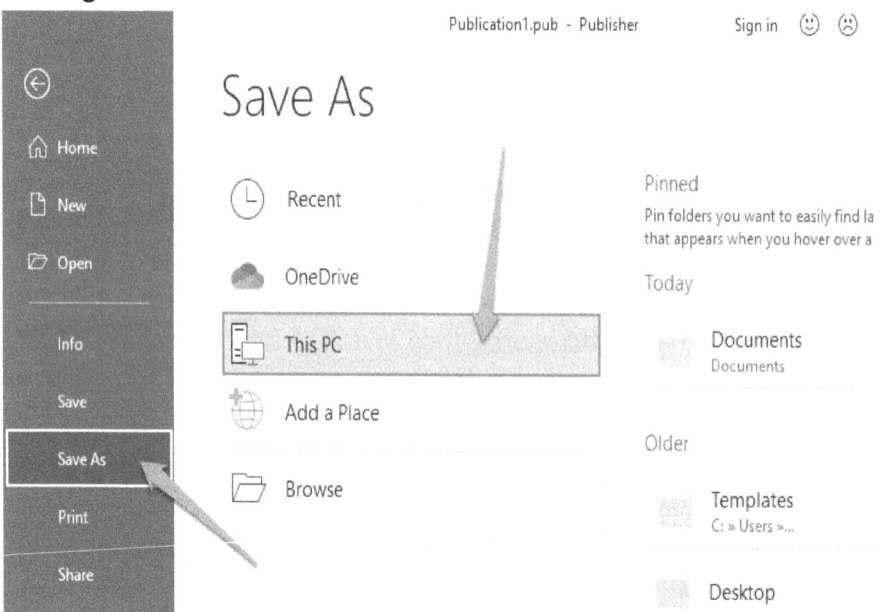

Name your file with a good name, in this event 'Birthday card'.

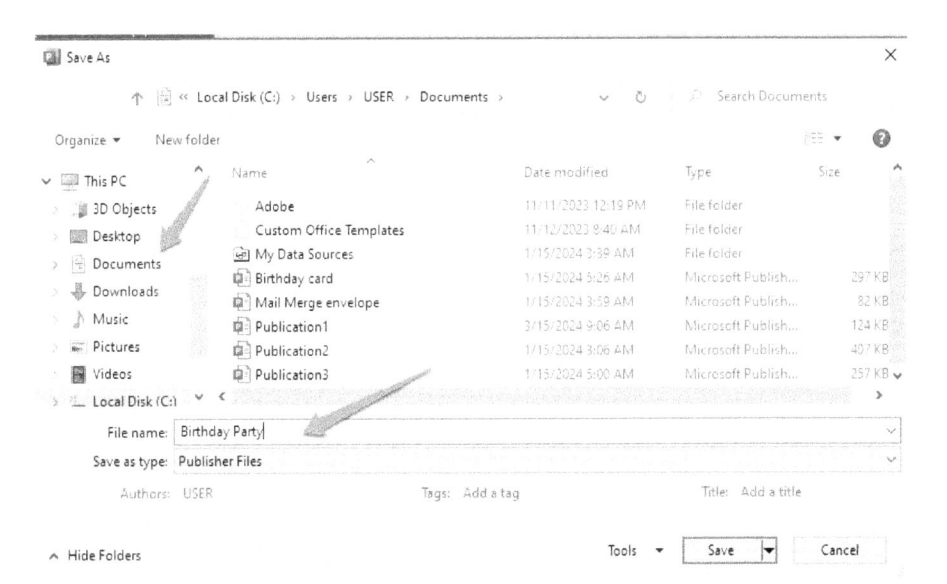

To alter the format, tick on the drop-down arrow in the field beneath, and from the list choose PDF.

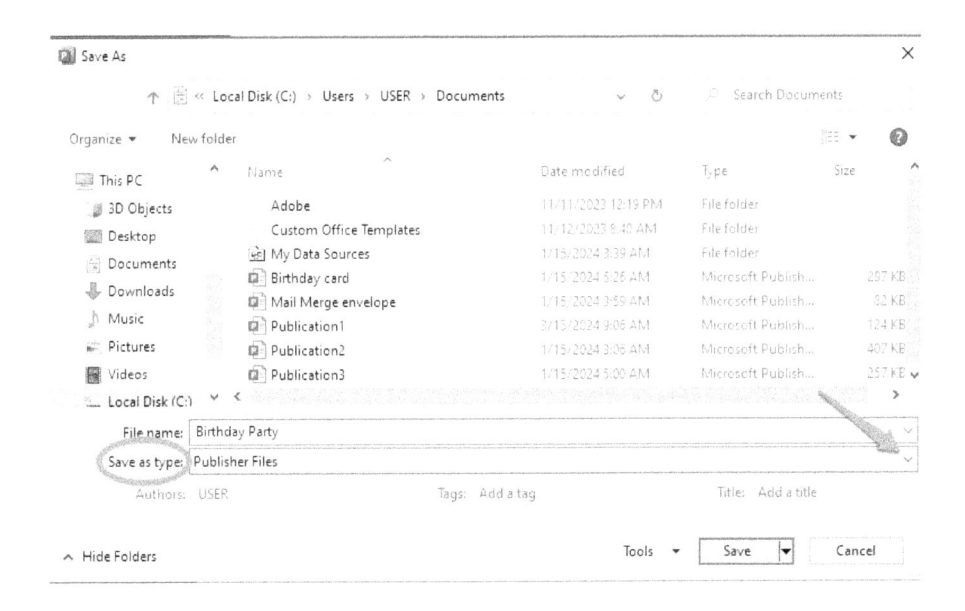

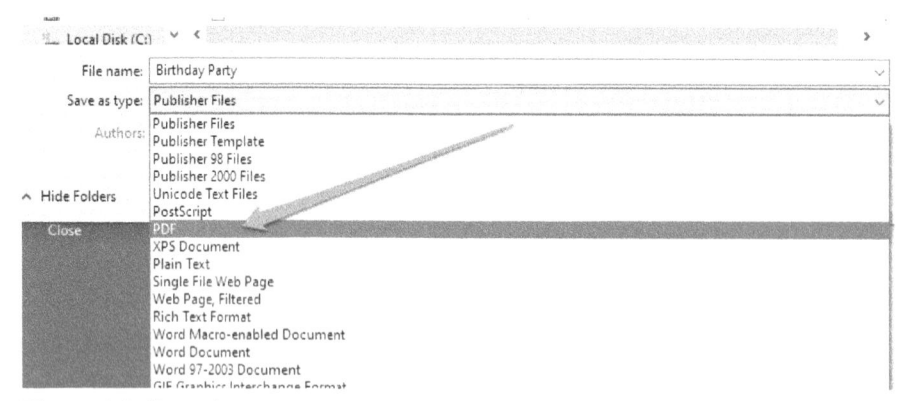

Then tick 'Save'.

How To Open Saved Documents

Supposing that you have already opened Publisher you can open previously or formerly saved documents, just tick on the 'file tab' on your screen at the top left side.

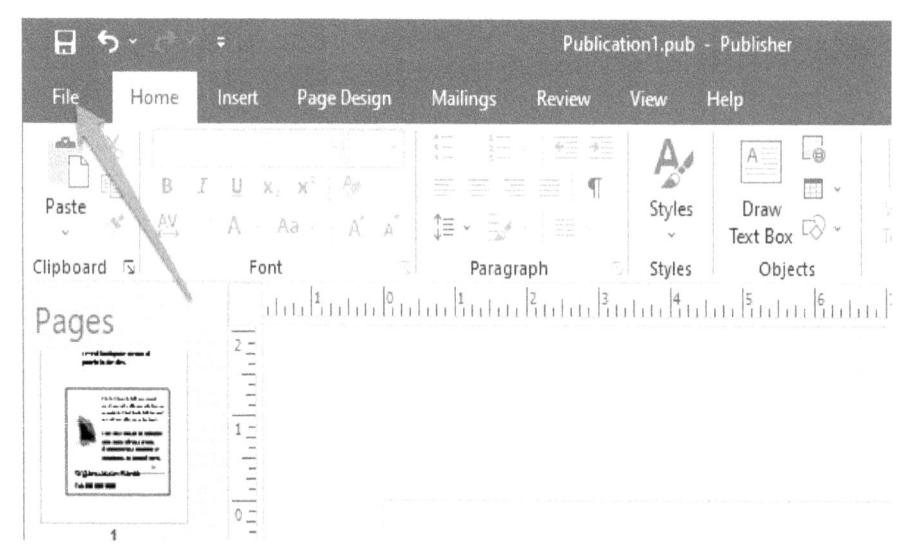

Tick 'open' from the green bar.

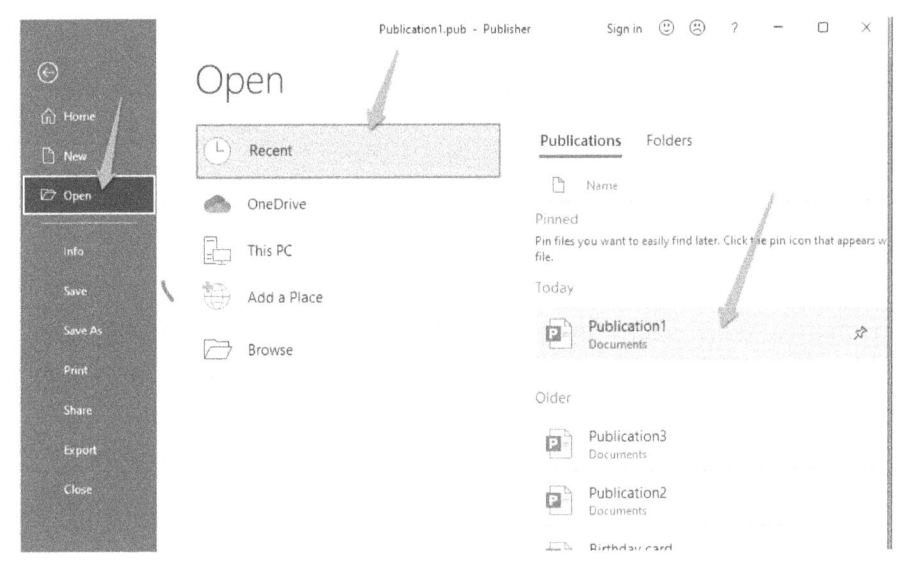

You can select the document you want to open from the list. The document from the former project was saved as 'Birthday card.pub', I will now open this specific one.

For easefulness, Microsoft Publisher specifies all your newly opened documents. The latest files will be specified first. Double-tap the file name to open it.

For example, if your document is saved on your PC, double-tap on the PC icon to survey the files. Select your file.

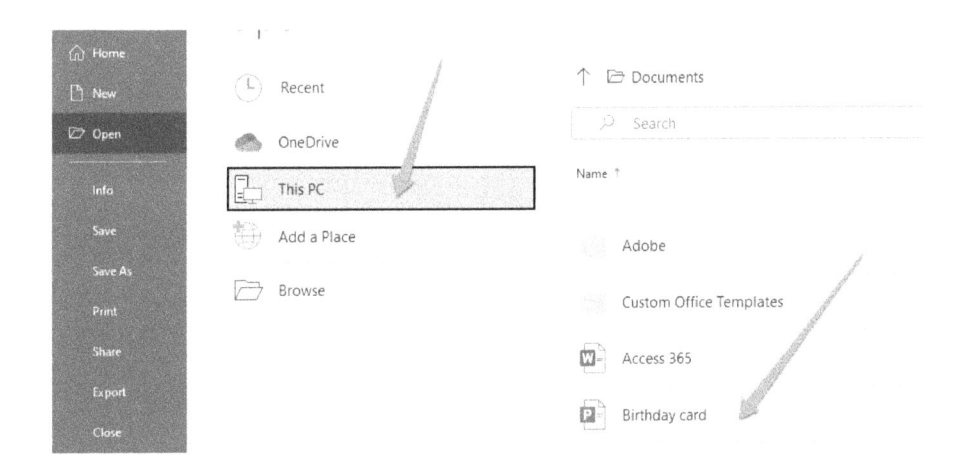

Tick 'open'.

Page Setup

Page setup allows you to change the paper size, orientation (portrait/landscape), margins, and general layout.

To change your page setup, drag to your 'page design' tab and choose the expand icon on the underside right of the page setup area.

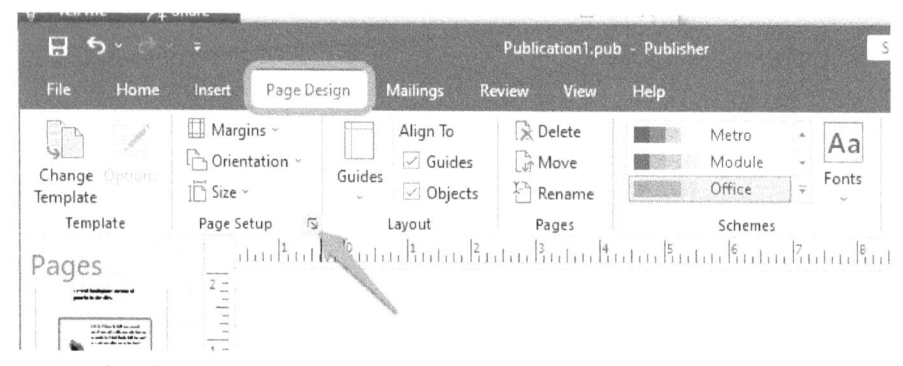

From the dialog box that appears, you can fix the layout type that is, you can make a booklet layout, full page, envelope, etc.

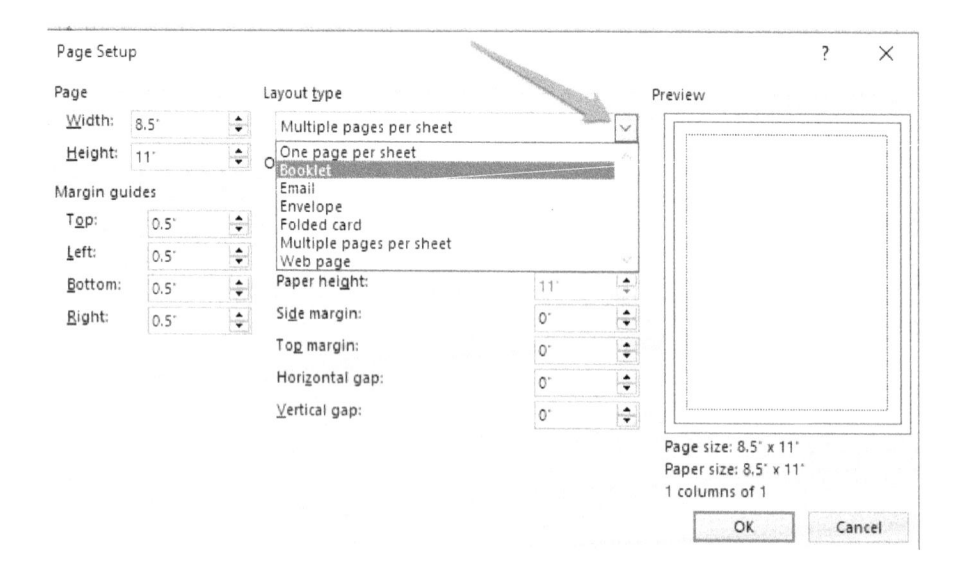

You can alter the margins as shown below by using the 'margin guide'.

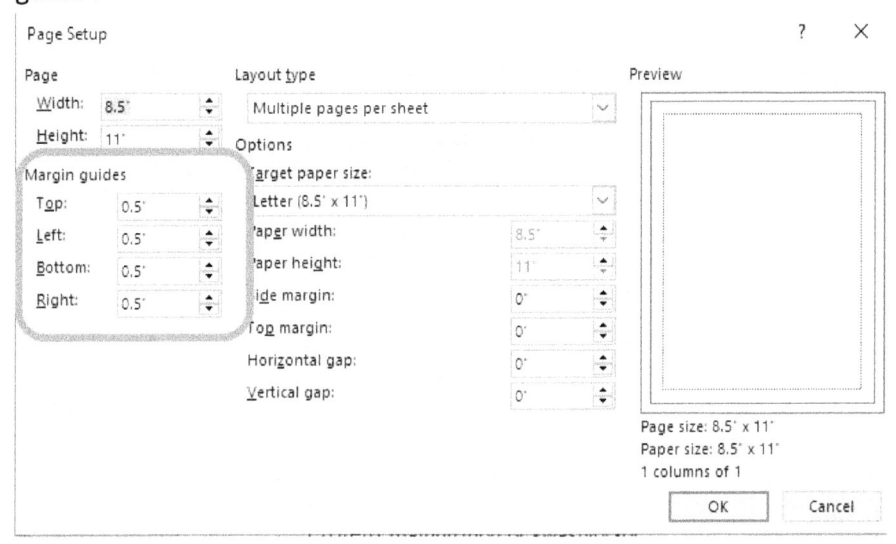

You can also alter the page scale.

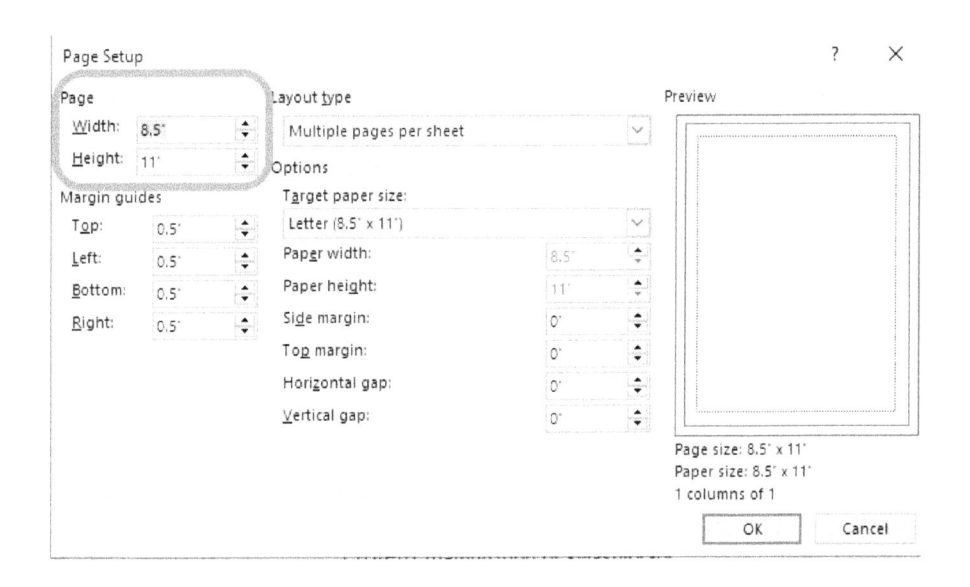

Producing Booklets

To produce a booklet layout, first, open a blank publication. From the page design tab, choose the icon at the bottom at the right of the 'page setup' area.

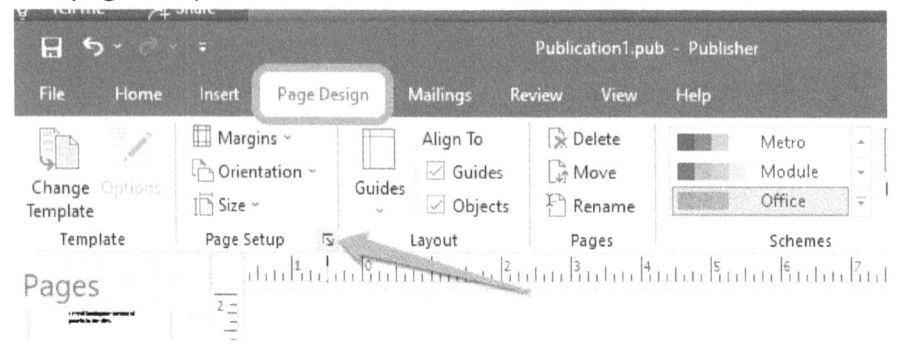

Choose 'booklet' in the 'page setup' dialog box, in 'layout type'.

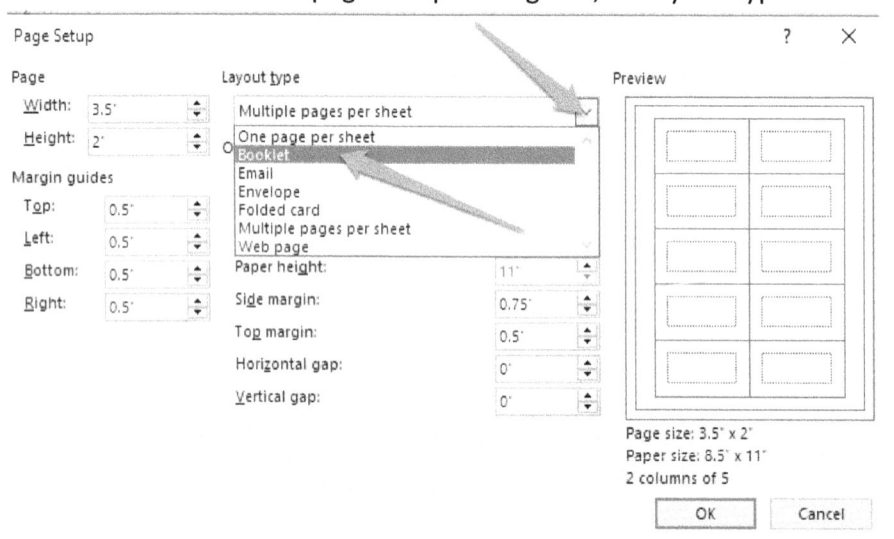

When you tick 'ok' the Publisher will produce a booklet layout for you. You will realize your pages in the navigation pane on the left-hand side of the screen. Here, you have your front page, the inside spread, and the back page.

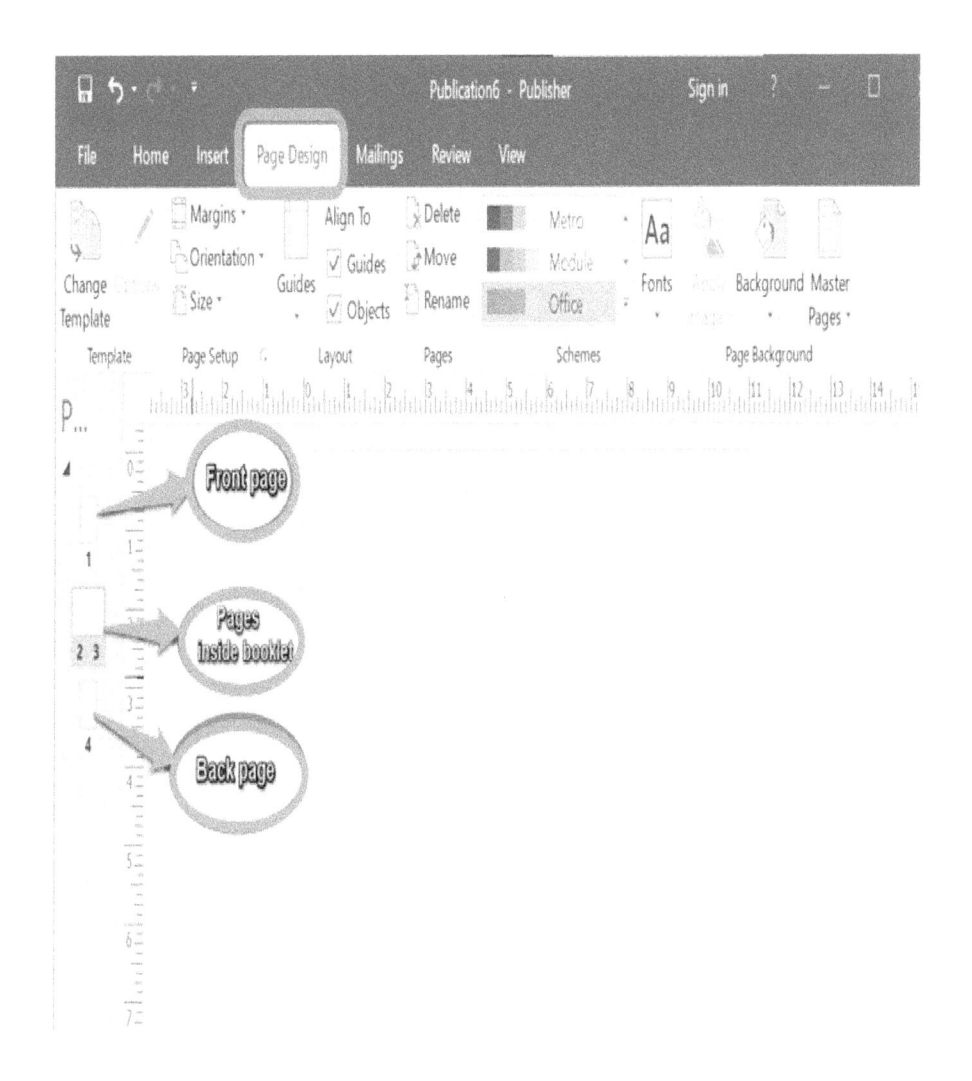

You can now commence producing your booklet. This is a suitable manner to commence. If you alter a Publisher document to booklet form you may face difficulty with the layout if the Publisher requires to rescale pages.

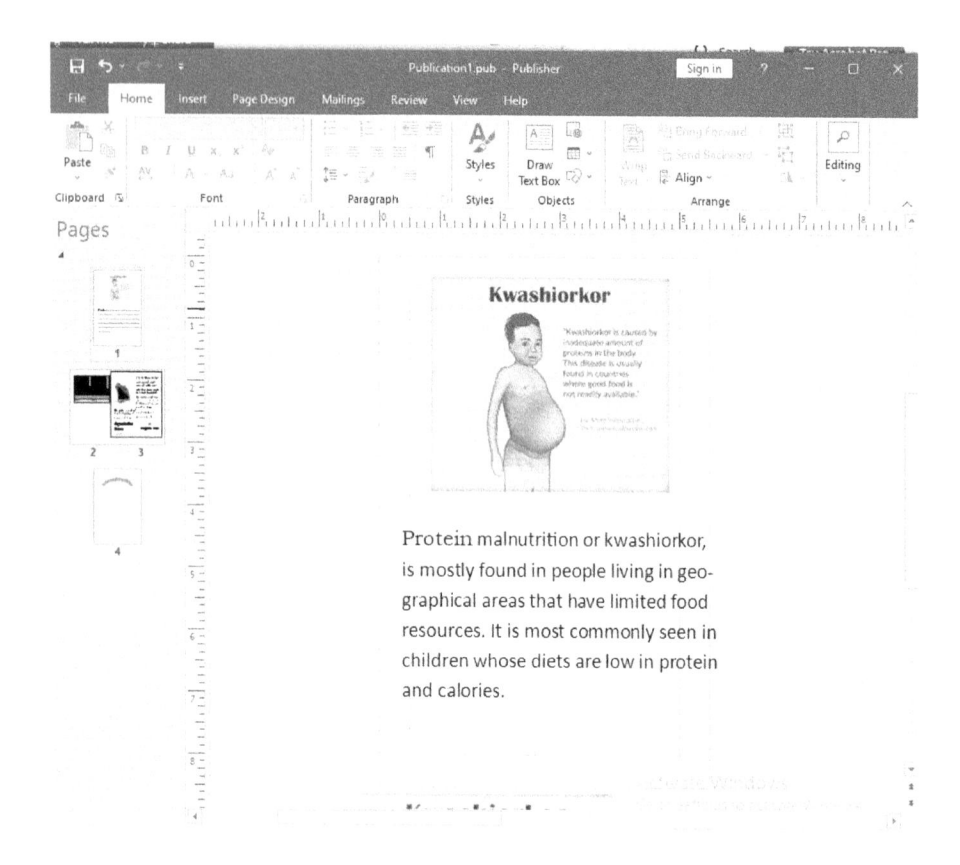

Making Use of Page Masters

Page Masters allows you to rerun layout elements and design on many pages in a publication. This leads to a more stable look all through your work and allows you to update the design in a single place, instead of altering them on each page.

Modifying Master Pages

For example, if you are producing a booklet, you can add page numbers or page headers on each page.

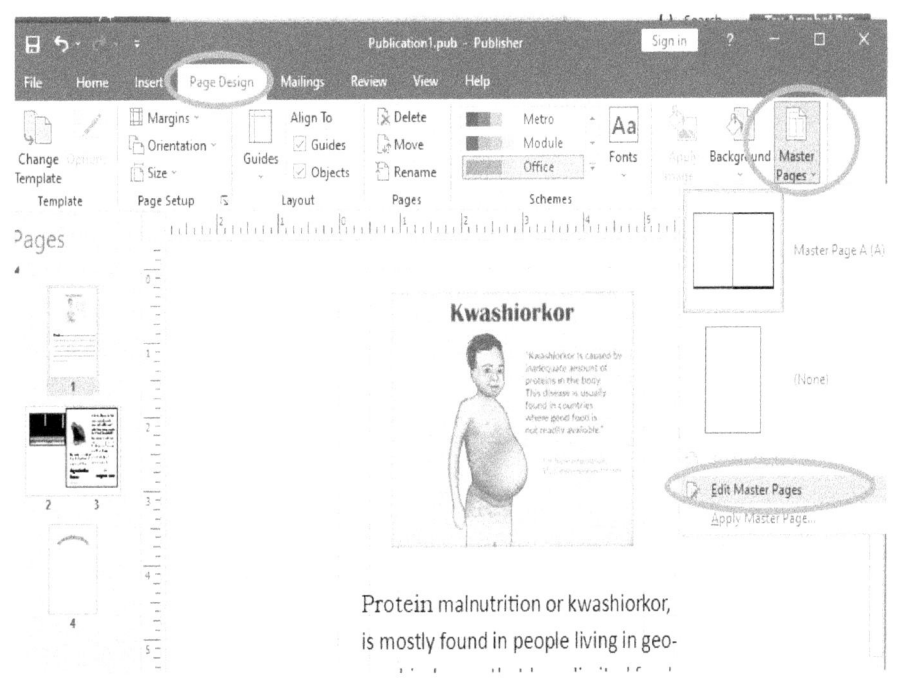

Attach a header such as a title

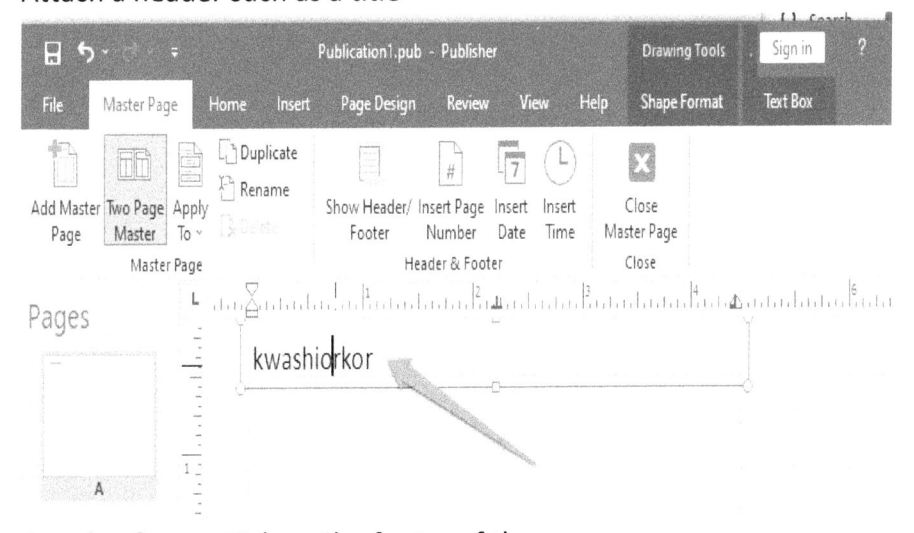

Attach a footer. Tick on the footer of the page.

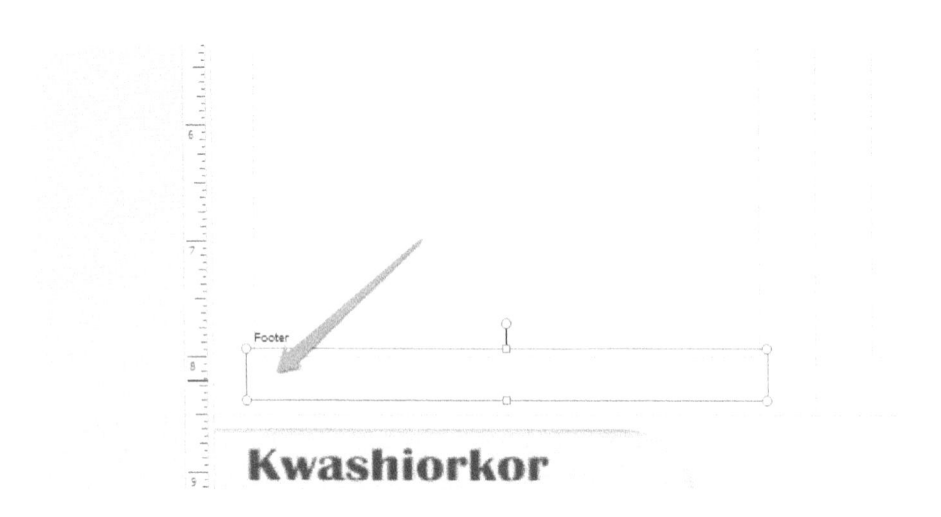

Attach the page number, and tick on the 'insert page number'.

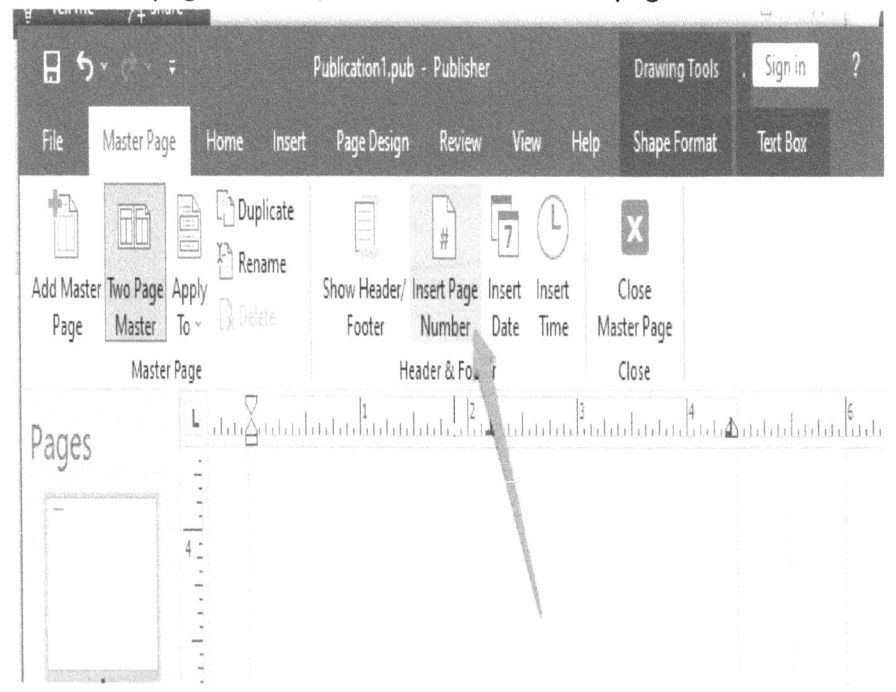

Producing Master Pages

To produce a new master, tick on the 'page design' tab, then choose 'add master page'.

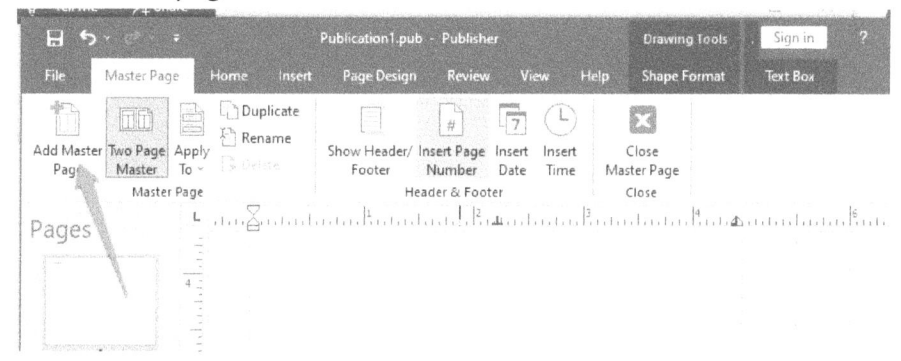

You can provide a descriptive name to the master in the 'description' area. Tick 'ok'.

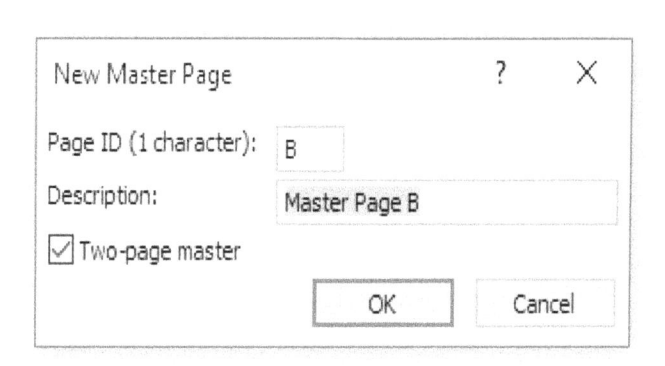

If you need the master to be a double-page spread, one you'd see in the middle of the booklet, tick 'two-page master'. If what you want is a separate page, un-tap this choice.

Produce your master now. You can insert text boxes or pictures as normal making use of the 'insert' tab.

Using Master

Right-click on the page or expand in the navigation pane on the left-hand side if you want to attach a master to a page. Scroll down to 'master pages' and select a master from the slideout options. If it is a master you want to use on many pages or a spectrum of pages, right-click on the page in the page navigation pane on the left. Move down to 'master pages', and choose 'apply master pages' from the slideout options. Choose the master you desire to use from the dialog box. Pick the pages you would like to apply the master too, eg 'all pages'. Tap 'ok'.

Putting In Guides

Layout guides allow you to stretch out your publication, text boxes, and align pictures, and tables. Layout guides appear on your page as a grid or line. There are specific guides you can use to develop your publication. To enable them, tick your 'page design' tab and choose 'guides'.

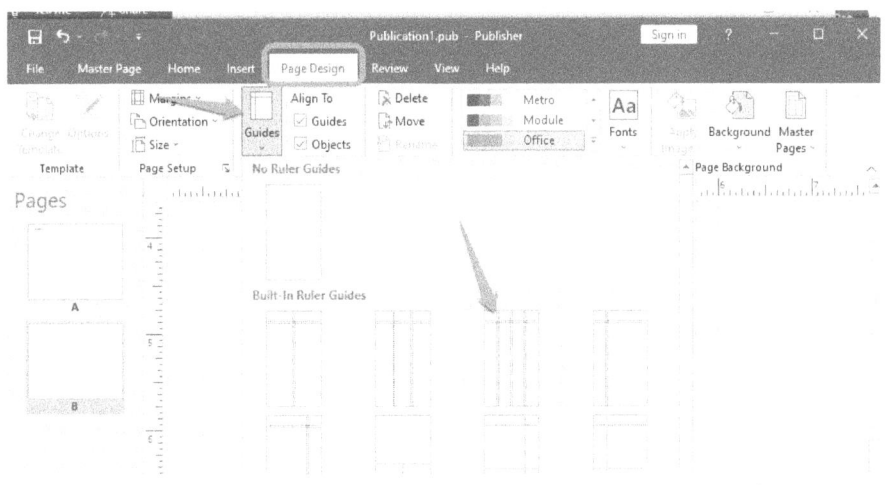

From the drop-down menu, you can select the setup you desire. For example, if you are establishing a newsletter pick a double or three-column setup. Organize your headings, text boxes, and pictures to the grid lines.

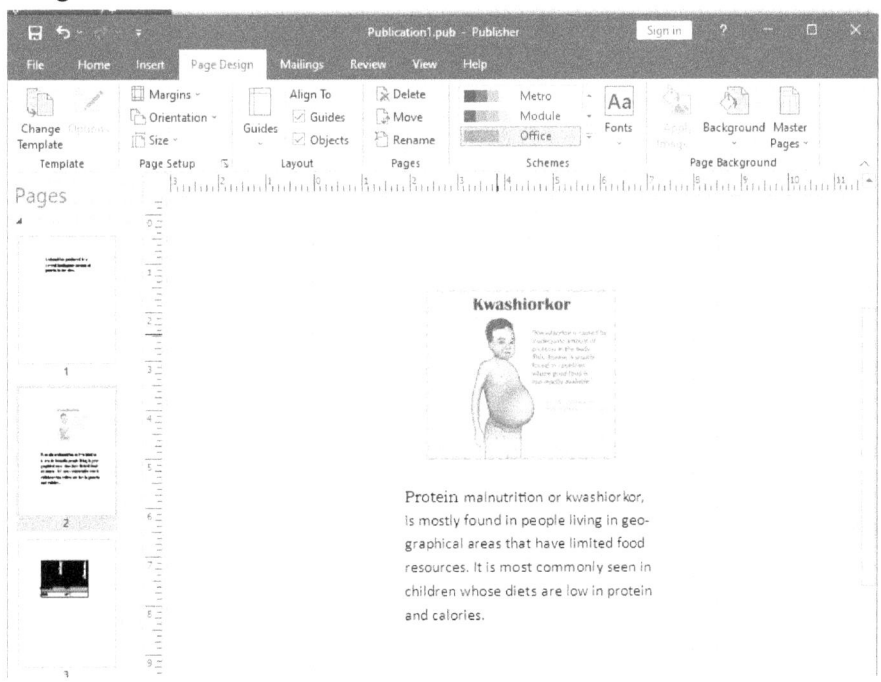

To display a setup line, tick and pull it to a new location.

Protein malnutrition or kwashiorkor,

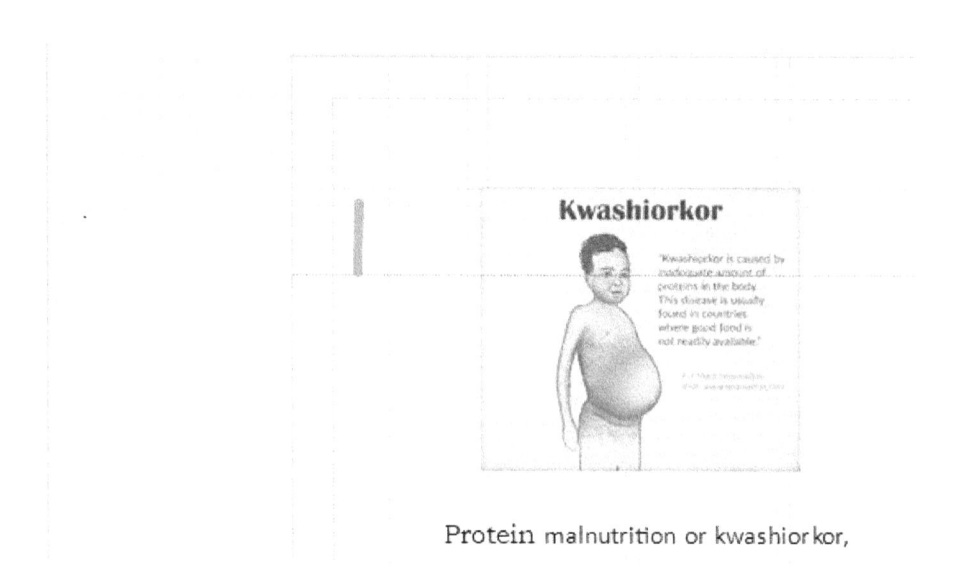

To attach a setup line, tick on the vertical ruler and move the green setup line into position on the page.

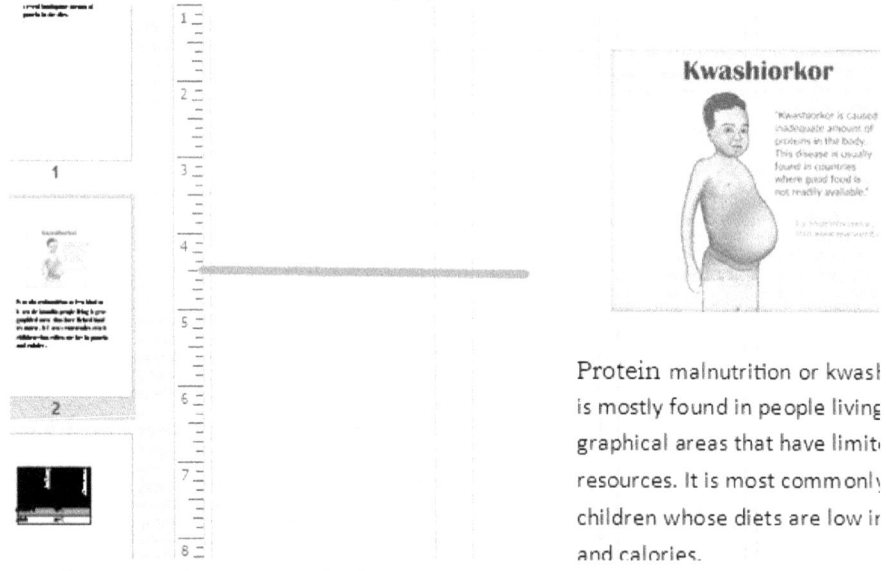

Protein malnutrition or kwasl
is mostly found in people living
graphical areas that have limite
resources. It is most commonly
children whose diets are low in
and calories.

For horizontal setup, tick the horizontal ruler and move the green down into position on the page.

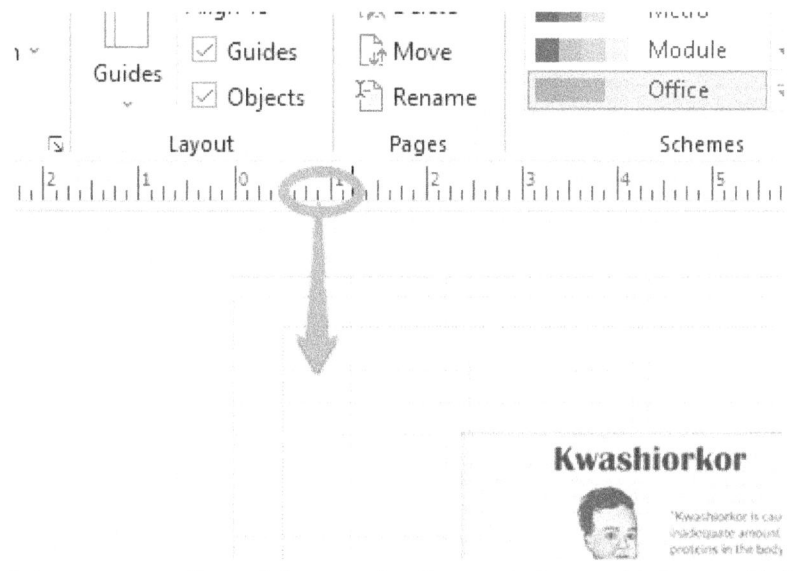

To delete a setup line, right-tap the line and choose 'delete guide'

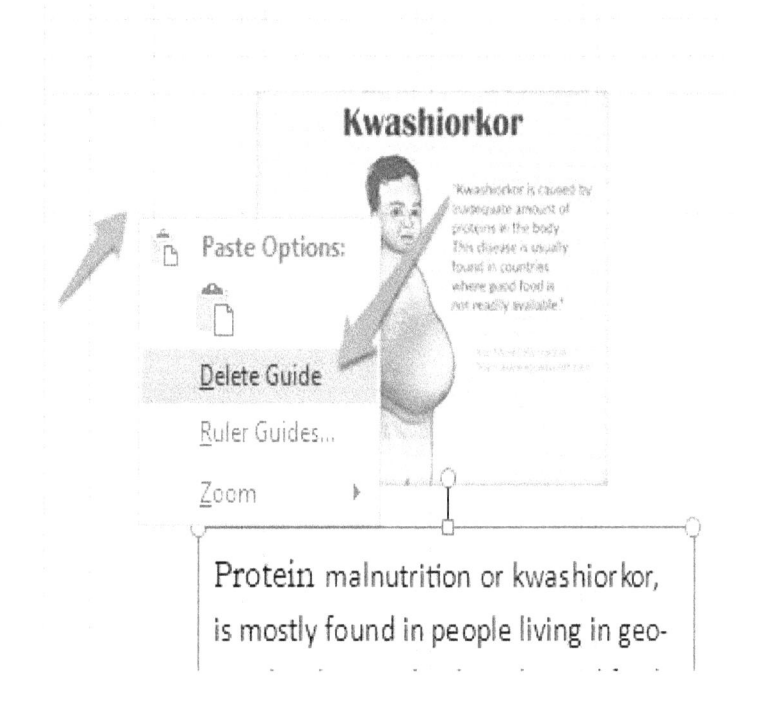

Chapter Seven
How To Publish Your Work

Do you want to be Published electronically? Printing? In this section, we will be taking a view at printing, exporting, and sharing your publication.

How To Print Your Documents

Tick 'file' on the top left of your screen.

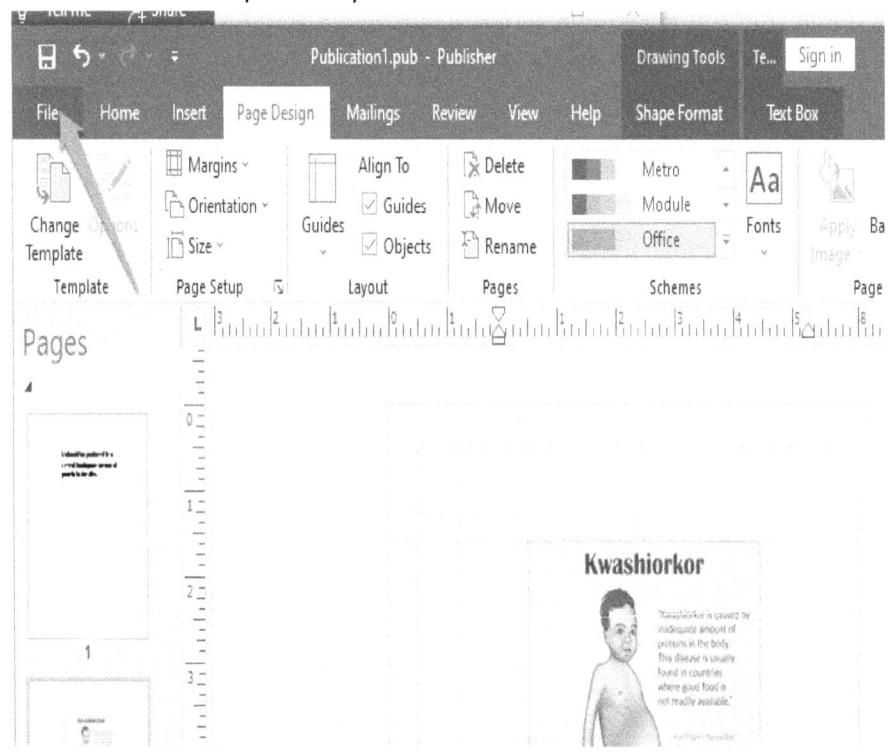

Select 'print' from the green bar on the left-hand side of the screen.

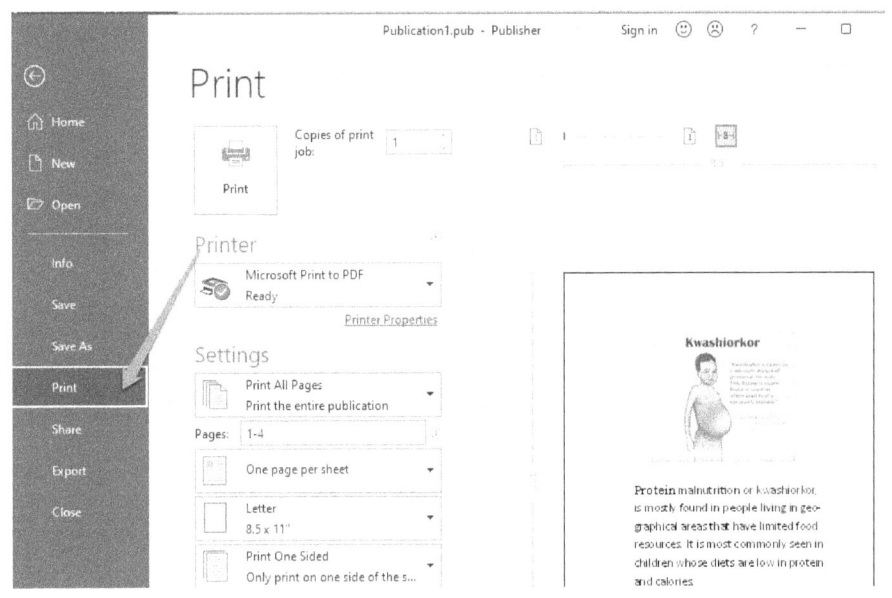

You can pick choices such as: printing individual pages or printing all pages and the number of copies. You can print many pages on a single sheet print the page on a single sheet of paper or scale it up to many sheets. You can also print the pages into a booklet. To change the setting tick the 'one page per sheet' drop-down menu.

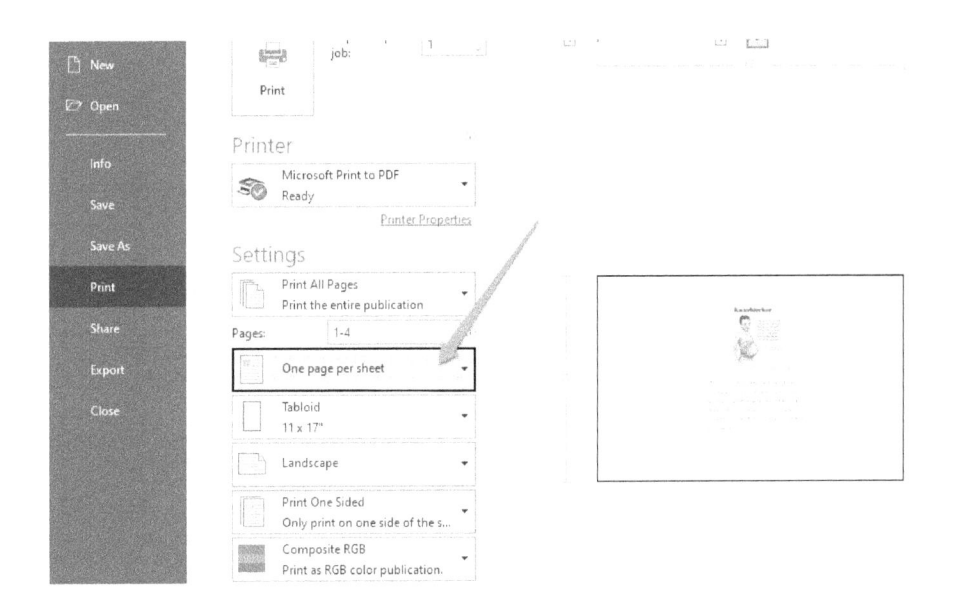

After you have picked all your options, tick the print button at the upper part.

Printing As a Booklet

Open your publication. Tick on the 'file' on the top left of the screen to print as a booklet.

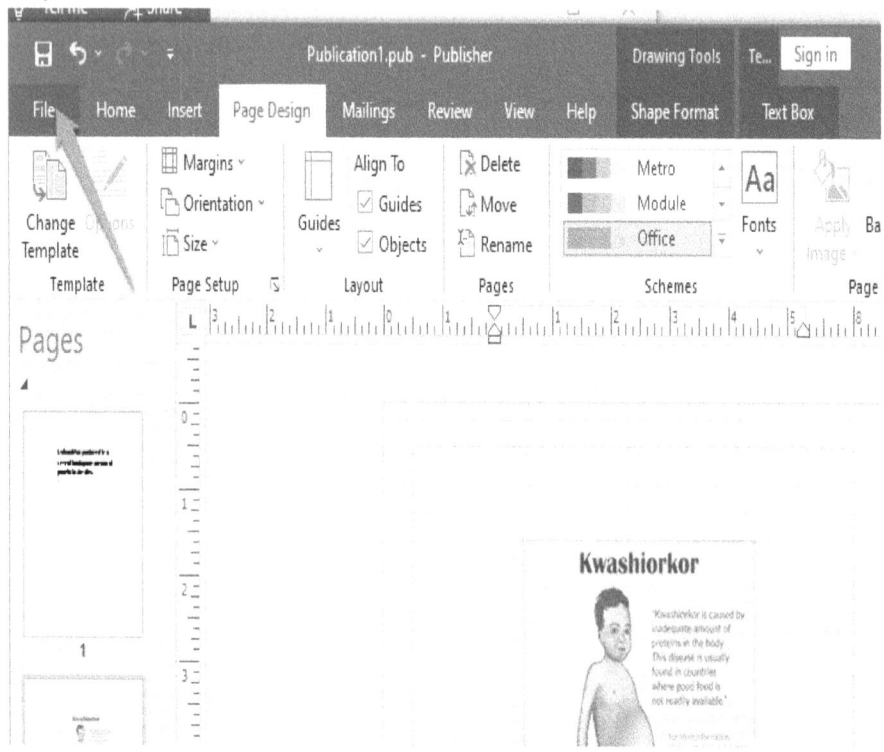

Tick 'print' from the green bar on the left-hand side of the screen.

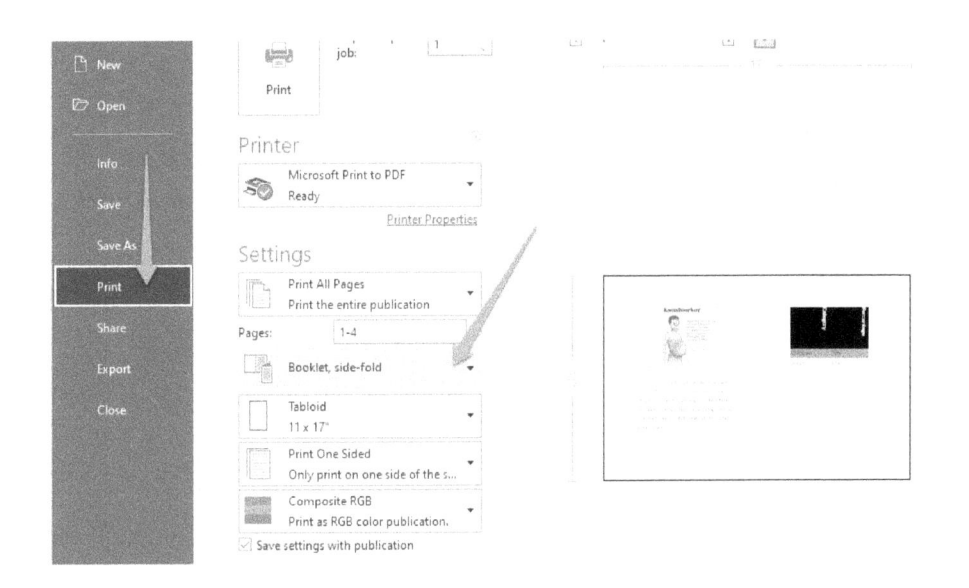

From the 'settings' section, go down to 'one page per sheet'. From the drop-down menu, pick 'booklet side fold'.

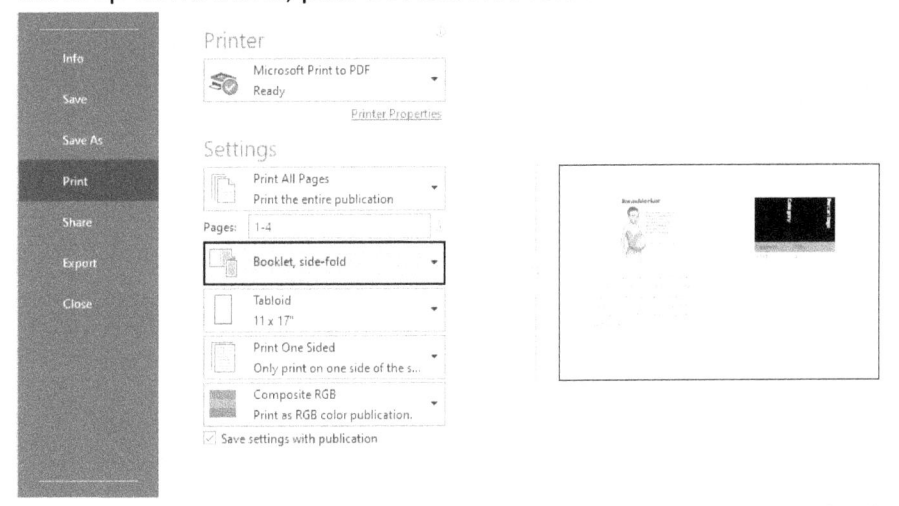

Most present printers allow double printing (i.e. printing on both sides of the paper). With various desktop printers, picking a duplex implies that the printer prints all the copies of the first side of a page, then halts and asks you to turn around the sheets that it just printed and put them back in the printer. Then all the copies of the second side would be printed.

To print on both sides, you have to tick on the drop-down box that says 'print one-sided'

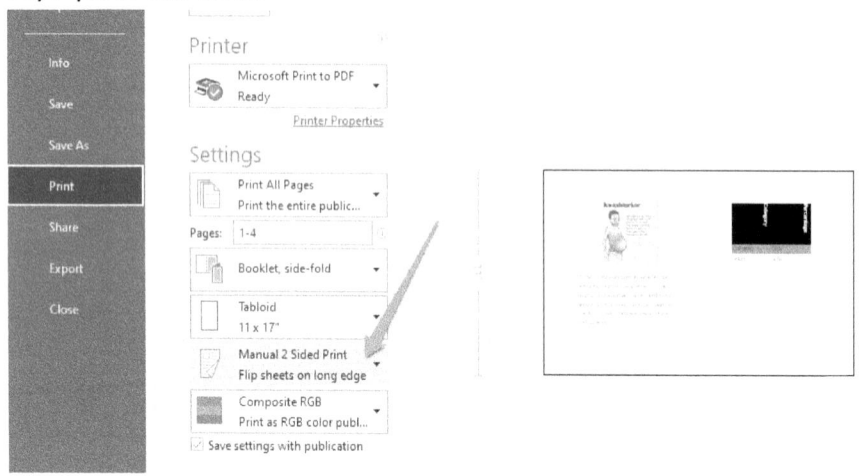

Tick 'print' at the topmost of the screen.

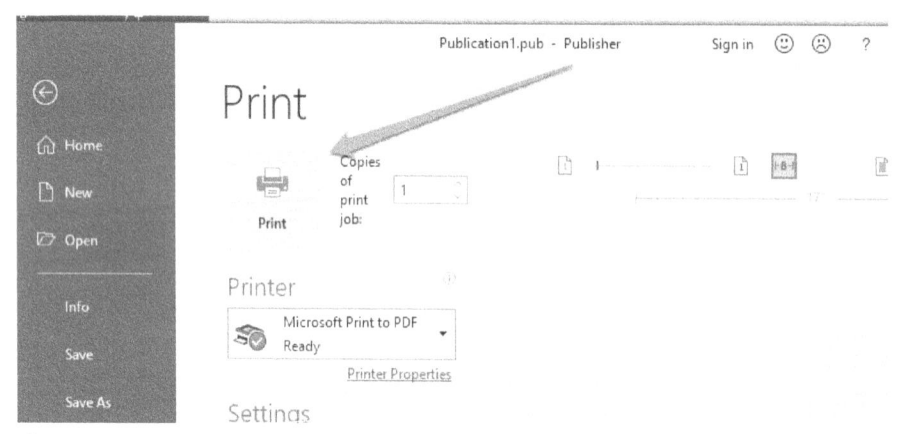

If you want to print on both sides of the page, instantly after the printer has printed the first page, turn the whole stack of the printed sheets over and put them back in the paper tray.

Exporting Your Work as a PDF

Tick on the file at the topmost left of your screen.

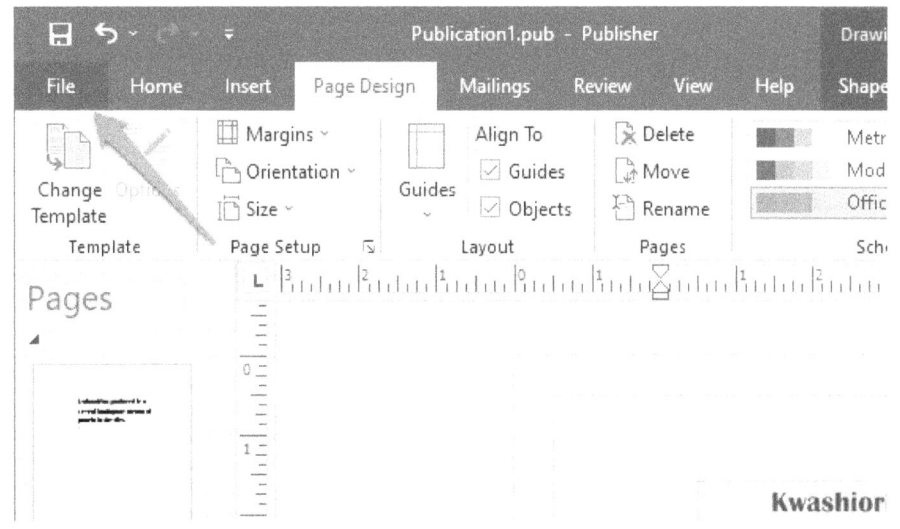

Pick 'export' from the left-hand side. Choose 'Create PDF/XPS Document', then tick on the 'Create PDF/XPS' button.

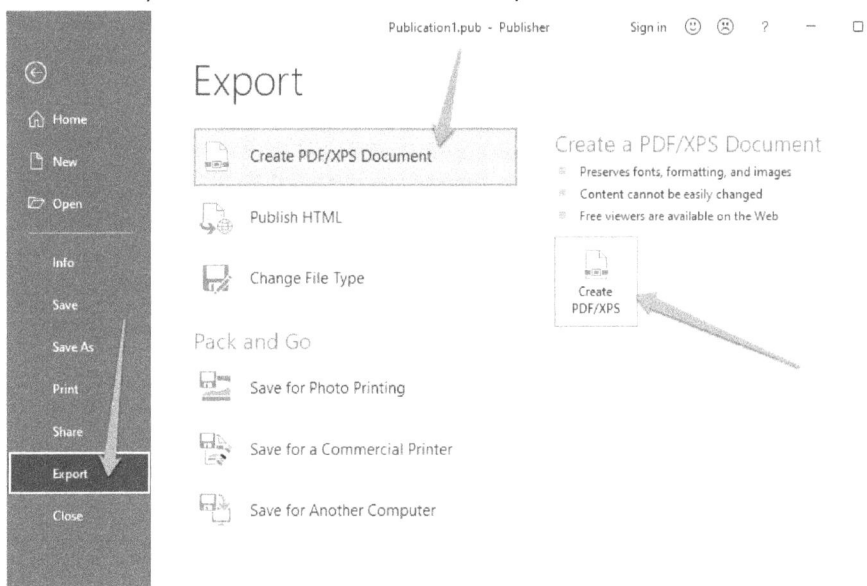

Select where you wish to store the PDF file, give it a meaningful name, then tick on 'publish'.

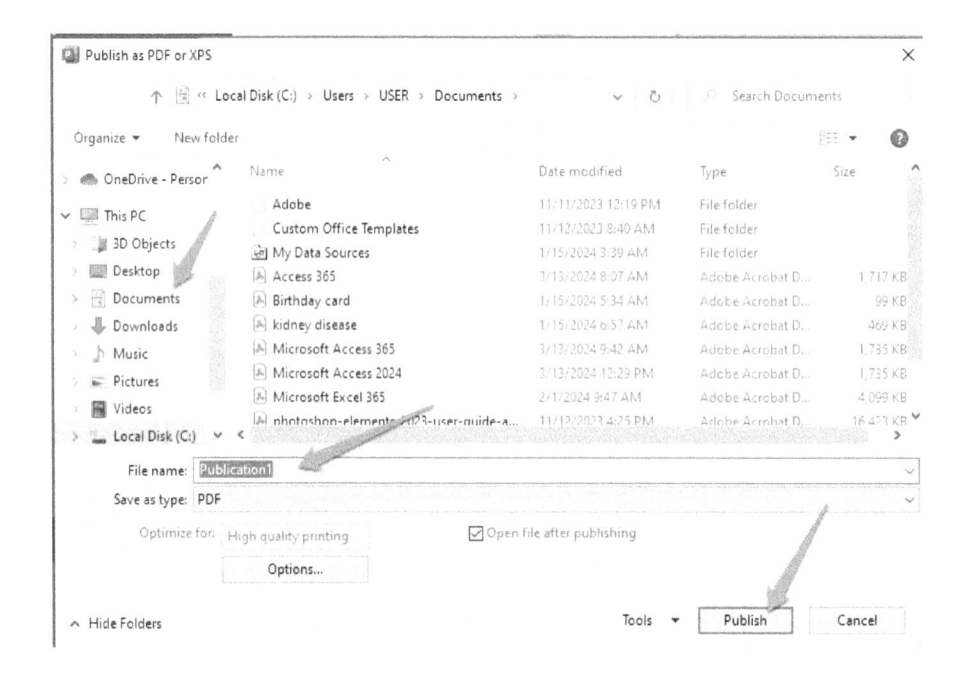

Sharing Of File

Tick the file on the left-hand side of the screen.

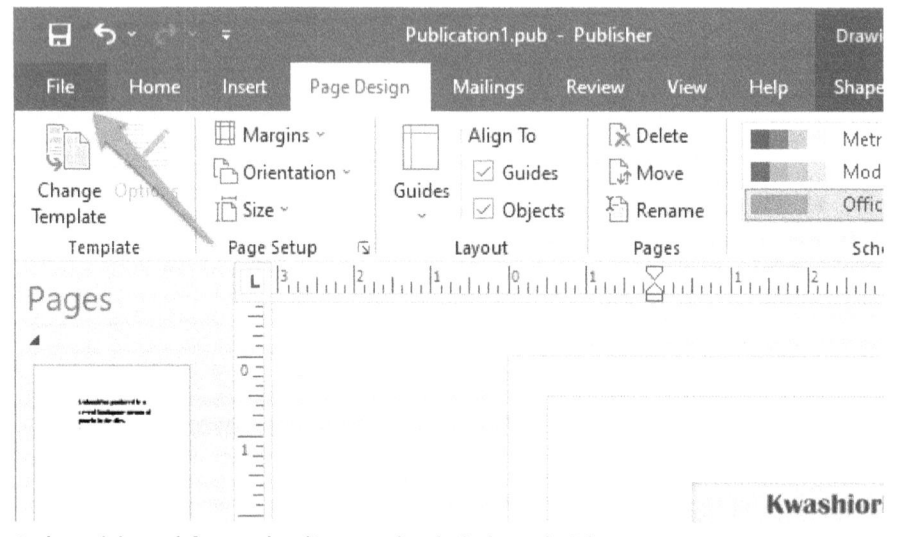

Select 'share' from the list on the left-hand side.

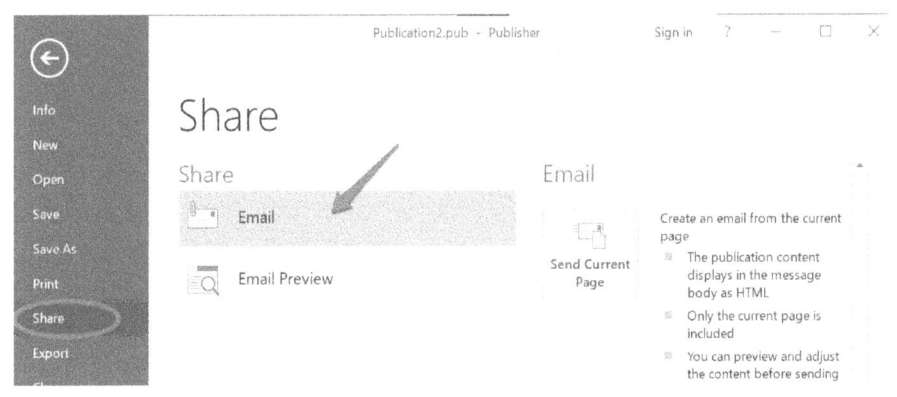

Choose how you want to connect the file to your email. You can send the newest page as an email, you can send your publication as a publisher file (.pub), and you can also transmit the file as a PDF. If you are transmitting the file to someone who doesn't have a publisher installed, you have to send the file as a PDF. For example, I want to send it as PDF. So I will have to tick 'send as PDF'. As soon as the email opens up, you will realize the file connected to the email. Attach the email address of the receiver and add a subject and a message.

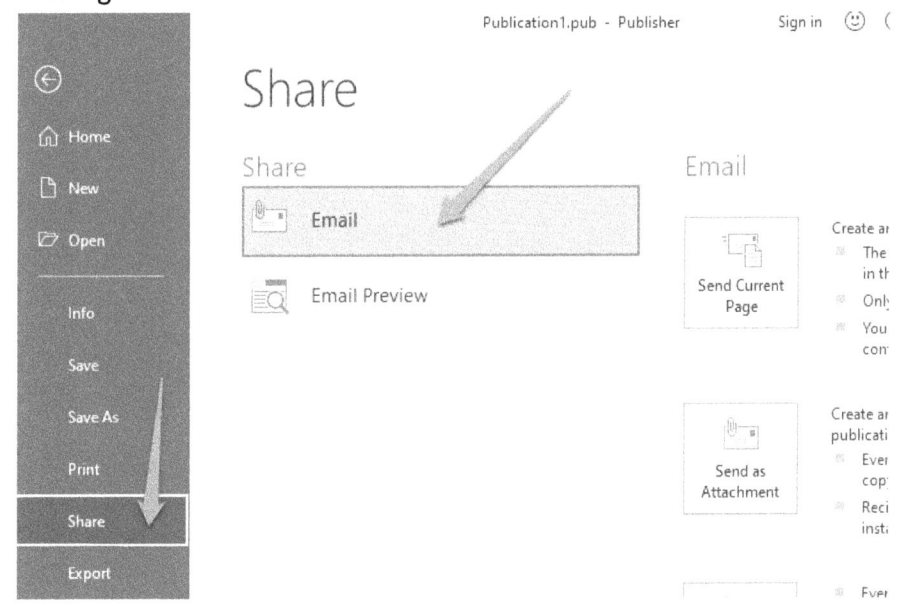

Tick 'send' when you are done.

CONCLUSION

I suppose you now have a detailed understanding of how to operate Microsoft Publisher after studying every part of this book, I am convinced you can now begin Publisher and find your way around the ribbon tab, and I also suppose you now know how to layout and design your page, format text such as bold, underlined, strike, and italic, use text boxes, use pre-designed templates, borders, accents, and page parts, change text color, use effects, build your templates, learn about typography, align text, add photos, wrap text, highlight text, and also cut, copy, paste, make use of the clipboard, crop, save your publication, convert your publications to other formats, and also how to print your publications.

INDEX

Adjusting Your Images, 82
Advertisements, 104
Alignment, 93
Altering Text Boxes, 47
blueprint, 103
Booklets, 134
Borders, 44
Borders and Accents, 101
Caption, 77
Cell Border, 64
clipart, 73
columns, 56
Cropping Images, 78
custom margins', 51
dialog boxes, 113
File Backstage, 14
Formatting, 58
home ribbon, 28
image thumbnail, 72
Inserting a Row, 60
Ligatures, 35
Mail Marge, 111
mailings, 116
Managing Publication, 126
Margins, 17
Merge cells, 62
Microsoft Publisher, 8
navigation pane, 140
Object Layers, 97
Objects Distribution, 94
Page Design Tab, 12
Page Masters, 136
Page parts, 97
placeholders., 98
Pre-designed, 122
Publication, 88
Publication Size, 16
review results', 115
Shadow, 91
single sheet, 145
Templates, 121
Text Autofit, 49
Text Direction, 67
Text Effects, 37
The Main Workspace, 18
The Ribbon Tabs, 11
Using Page Setup, 132
WordArt, 106
WordArt styles, 39
Working Graphics, 69
WORKING WITH GUIDES, 21
Wrapping Text, 85